Barney and Molly:

A True Dublin Love Story

by

Martin Duffy

Ogma Press

Copyright Martin Duffy 2006
First published by Ogma Press N.Y. 2006
ISBN-10: 0-9785853-1-3
ISBN-13: 978-0-9785853-1-0
All rights are reserved by the author.
For further info visit www.duffyberlin.com
For distribution visit www.ogmapress.com

Contents

Introduction- vii
Who's Who- xi

The Book:

How the Duffys and Dowdalls Teamed Up-1
A Young Family in Dublin's Inner City-20
11, Brabazon Street-37
A New Life in Crumlin-47
Hard Life and Holes in Pockets-58
Four Generations-71
The Fifties Begin-86
The Change of Life is Kicking-98
Workers and Children-115
The Scattering Begins-131
Crumlin in London-148
The End of the Fifties-165
The Sixties-181
The Chain is Broken-194
New Life and Love-207
Father of the Brides-225
From Grand Canal to Swimming Pool-244
Story's End-256
Kevin Tammany Duffy-276
The Reunion-282

Introduction

Molly's 80th birthday, on April 12th 1987, had passed quietly. Some of her daughters had visited her during the day, and naturally there had been a stream of phone calls. But by evening time she was alone, as usual, in her home at 147 Leighlin Road in Crumlin.

The house, with two bedrooms upstairs and a livingroom, scullery, and built-on kitchenette downstairs, had long ago hummed with life as Molly and her husband Barney raised their thirteen children. The piano in the livingroom had been the centre of song and laughter when her brother Willie had visited. The house had been the home of bare-foot children through the struggles of the Forties. In the Fifties there was one son disassembling his motorbike, another winning armloads of trophies for running, the teddy boy getting in trouble with his parents and the police again, while the daughters sat around together making dresses to go ballroom dancing. In the Sixties, it was the hub for a string of marriages as the family expanded to a new generation so that the home would yet again surge with life on Sunday afternoons when children and grandchildren gathered around Barney and Molly. There had been tears and laughter, love and heartbreak. There had been family life in all its glory.

On this night, however, the house was silent but for the sound from the television as Molly sat alone half drowsing.

Then her son-in-law Derek Carruthers called to the door. Molly's daughters Brigid and Ethel had invited her to join them for a drink as a last celebration to end the day. Molly didn't drink alcohol, but she was happy to go along. She was a little surprised that Derek was driving so far away - not to a pub around Walkinstown where Brigid lived, but instead out to Tallaght and the barn-sized pub that was The Embankment.

When they arrived at the car park, Derek helped Molly out of the car. She had been a strong woman, but in recent years had grown frail. She now, after a hip replacement operation, even needed a walking frame. Derek slowly led her inside and along the corridor, but instead of leading her to the lounge he led her to the hall where events like wedding parties usually took place.

As she arrived at the door of the hall, music struck up - 'Happy Birthday to you...' Molly was greeted by the sight of close to two hundred people waiting there to greet her. Eleven of her twelve living children - including Bill, who had flown in from Canada; Luke and Peter, who had flown in from England; and Marie Duffy, the widow of her late son. Assembled also were Molly's grandchildren and great-grandchildren and the spouses and partners. It was the tribe to which this extraordinary woman had given birth, and all had gathered to celebrate Molly and their love for her.

There is a video of the party. In the course of the evening, one by one everyone came to pay homage to Molly. What is most striking about the video is to see how much love Molly showed - especially for the children. All were kissed and hugged and listened to.

Her smile was full of love, and she delighted in being surrounded by her family.

It was the last big celebration of Molly's life. Three years later, after a long illness, she died and the family gathered to mourn her. But her life, and that of her husband Barney, was a story that spanned most of twentieth century Dublin and is rich in tall tales and true of their tragedies and triumphs. This book is an attempt to tell the story of Barney and Molly Duffy in the hope that future generations will know, and be rightfully proud of, the remarkable man and woman from whom they stem.

Barney and Molly were two ordinary people who lived extraordinary lives. Their marriage was a shared journey that tested and proved, time and again, the power of their love. They were the finest of Dublin working class people, devoted to each other and to their children. This book is a celebration of Barney and Molly.

We are all born into a story that has run before us and will run after us. We want to know the story we have inherited.

I was born into an epic - a wonderland of stories - which I am sure is why I became a storyteller. When I was a kid of twelve or so, I asked for and was given a typewriter for Christmas. This was a toy typewriter that you twisted a knob on to turn to one letter after the next and then slapped down the bar to strike that letter through an ink ribbon onto the page. With that typewriter, I produced 'The Duffy News' - our family newspaper. I produced a few issues - I remember even posting copies to family in London. Moving on forty or so years, I am now writing a book that will pass on down the generations as a record of our parents and their lives and how we all came into the world and grew up. A book full of our memories and memories of our parents. A story well and truly worth telling!

Writing this book has turned out to be for me, the youngest sibling and some kind of accidental afterthought in the family, a chance to connect with my parents and brothers and sisters. I hope that I can be a link between the generation of my brothers and sisters and the generations to come. Just as I was born already an uncle, maybe I was born already destined to pass the great story of this family on. I am happy and honoured to do so.

And now, on with the book and I must swap over from writing in first-person to joining everyone else in the third-person narrative. So when you later read my writing about myself in the third person, it's not that I am yet again proving my brother Kevin's opinion that I was always odd. I am simply taking my place in the epic.

Let the story begin.....

Martin Duffy

Who's Who...

There is a fine tradition in the family of passing names on down the generations, but this can also lead to some initial confusion in reading the book. Below is a simple line-up of the cast of characters in relation to the central figures of our story; *BARNEY DUFFY* and *MOLLY DOWDALL*.

BARNEY DUFFY;
Barney's father was *PATRICK AMBROSE DUFFY*. Patrick Ambrose was married three times. His first wife was Josephine, his second Ellen and his third Peg. Barney's mother was *ELLEN DUFFY*.

Patrick Ambrose and Ellen had six children;

PETER, BERNARD (BARNEY), PADDY, ELLEN, JOHN, KEVIN.

MOLLY DOWDALL;
Molly's parents were *LUKE* and *ELIZABETH DOWDALL*.

Luke and Elizabeth had six children;

> *MARY (MOLLY), MARGARET, LILY, LUKE, DELIA, WILLIAM.*

Molly's parents were always called *MOTHER DOWDALL* and *FATHER DOWDALL* by Barney and Molly's children and after their introduction in the book are referred to only as such.

Molly's uncle Benny Dowdall, would return to the story in the 1950s.

One brother of Molly's, William (Willie) Dowdall, remained in constant contact with the family.

THE CHILDREN OF BARNEY AND MOLLY;

Barney and Molly repeated almost all the family names with their children.

BARNEY and MOLLY's children were;

Ellen, Elizabeth (Betty), Bernard, Maureen, Bernadette (Breda), Luke, Margaret (Greta), Peter, Patrick (Paddy), William (Willie), Brigid, Bernard*, Kevin, Ethel, Martin.

* events in the book explain this repetition.

Barney
&
Molly

How the Duffys and Dowdalls Teamed Up

This book is about Barney and Molly, but the clans and family names of the couple are worth a brief introduction as part of their stories.

The Duffy clan is Northern Irish - Duffy is the most common name in County Monaghan. The Irish for the name - O'Dubhthaigh - comes from 'dubh', the Irish for black, and other possible connections including 'the black/foreign man' or 'the people of peace'. The name has a long association with clergy, both pagan and Catholic. The first Druid to convert to Saint Patrick's Christianity, for instance, was named Dubhthach. He is the patron saint of Donegal.

Barney's father, Patrick Ambrose Duffy, was a fine strong handsome man with bright blue eyes, a mass of ginger hair, and a wide moustache. He prided himself in always being immaculately groomed. He was a charming and lively man who lived a rich and adventurous life. He was born on December 6th 1876 in Annyart, in the district of the townland Castleblayney, County Monaghan. His birthplace borders Muckno Lake. His father's name was Patrick Duffy - described as a labourer - and his mother's name was Margaret. Her maiden name was Tomaney. The child's birth was registered a week after his birth by a Mary Tomaney. On the birth certificate is an X, and beside it the statement 'this is the mark of Mary Tomaney, present at birth' - in other words, she was illiterate. These were humble beginnings for a man who would father the male lead of the Duffy family story. Patrick Ambrose, born less than thirty years after the end of the Great Famine that halved Ireland's population, was the genetic bridge leading this Duffy family to Dublin and beyond.

Patrick Ambrose Duffy

Patrick Ambrose became a gardener and was married three times. The marriage to his first wife, Josephine, cannot be traced. But it did not happen in Monaghan, so the man had already begun his life of wandering the country following his trade. He had a daughter from this marriage, Maggie - named after his mother. Josephine died - presumably not very long after the birth of the daughter. It is quite possible, given the times, that the woman even died in childbirth. There are gaps and mysteries in Patrick Ambrose's life before he settled in Dublin. It is known that he took the brave decision of keeping his daughter and carrying on his work, travelling around Ireland as a gardener for hire. He would usually have worked on the estates of the British gentry.

The second wife of Patrick Ambrose was Ellen Farrell. It is unclear if she was from Tipperary or Kildare. There is no record of where he met her or where (and hence when) they married.

With her he had a daughter, Ellen, and five sons; Peter, Bernard, Paddy, John and Kevin. Patrick Ambrose travelled around the country to find work, and as a result the children were born in different counties. Bernard - Barney - was born in Waterford, on Sunday July 19th 1903, at a time when his parents were living in the gate lodge of an estate called Saint Patrick's. He inherited his father's light blue eyes which, set against his dark features, added to his good looks. His sister Ellen - who was known as Nellie - was born in Wexford. Kevin, the youngest, was born May 13th 1913 in Dromond, County Wicklow. Kevin was given the middle name 'Tammany' - which would indicate a confusion on Patrick Ambrose's behalf regarding the spelling of his own mother's maiden name. His intention must have been to preserve his mother's family name - which was not an unusual tradition - but presumably by then he had heard of Tammany Hall in New York, a seat of corrupt political power that was mostly run by the Irish. The 'Tammany' in that instance, however, is from the name of a Native American chief.

The family moved into Dublin city - to Brabazon Street, off the Coombe. It was probably around this time that Patrick Ambrose worked as a foreman gardener in Phoenix Park. The Coombe was part of what was known as The Liberties - one of the first areas housing people outside the walls of Dublin city. The Coombe was not far from the Guinness brewery and down the road from a slaughterhouse, the two smells competing with each other. The area teemed with the harsh tenement life of a fading capital city that had once been considered the second city of the United Kingdom but had fallen into decay since the Act of Union that was brought in by the British in 1800 in a further effort to tame the colonised Irish.

1916 was the year of the Easter Uprising, and during that war Barney - thirteen years old - was a messenger running from the rebel base at Boland's Mills near Dublin's Ringsend. This is where Barney's lifetime hero, Eamon de Valera, was in command. That rebellion had been swiftly crushed by the British, but the brutality of their victory and Catholic Ireland's persistent determination to gain freedom led to negotiations between the Irish rebels and the British. De Valera - 'Dev', as he came to be known - was originally sentenced to death like the other leaders of the rebellion. This, however, was commuted to life imprisonment. Dev was released the following year and was elected head of the Sinn Fein (Irish for 'ourselves alone') Party that would lead the political struggle for independence. He would later end up interned in England and escaping from there in these colourful early years of his life as Ireland's great leader.

How the Duffys and Dowdalls Teamed Up

Barney, during this time, had been working as a messenger boy for the company PJ Byrne, 'saw maker and repairer', on Drury Street. He quit this job in July 1918 and was given the following reference; 'Bernard Duffy has been in my employment as general messenger for the past two years. During that time he collected many of my accounts and proved himself strictly honest and always ready to oblige. He leaves now at his own request having given due notice of his intention. I would be glad to recommend him to any person requiring a Steady Boy'.

He later worked for Hugh Brady, family grocer, on Bridge Street. Leaving there in June 1919, his employer gave him a reference describing him as 'sober, honest, and attentive to his work'.

By 1922, the streets of Dublin were full of danger. A Treaty had been signed between the Irish and the British accepting the partition of the mainly Protestant Northern Six Counties in return for independence for the rest of the island. De Valera quit as leader of the main Irish party, Sinn Fein, and formed a new Republican Party. Attempts were made to find agreement between de Valera and Michael Collins - who was then heading a Provisional Government that would oversee the British withdrawal from the twenty six counties. But talks failed and Civil War broke out. Barney Duffy was very much on de Valera's side, although no one knows how active he was for the cause during this time.

The Irish were now fighting between themselves as well as against the British still on their soil. One time, Barney was playing cards with a group of men in Summerhill and one of the men was shot dead by the

British. After the incident, it was discovered that the victim was in the British army and was home on leave. The British then wanted to give him a military funeral. They were warned by the dead man's family not to dare add that insult to the murder.

Barney's brother Kevin was a young boy growing up on the streets of Dublin as the English rag-tag army known as the Black and Tans were patrolling the streets. The British had said that these were an 'auxiliary military police', but in fact they were dedicated to hunting down Republicans and so were hated by the people. In around the Coombe, the Black and Tans had a system; they would come down the hill to the intersection with Meath Street and halt there to disperse.

Kevin had a friend, Christy Murphy, and they would go into an abandoned public house that was near this corner and would gather up stones and bricks.

"As soon as they stopped," he recalled, "we used to pelt them with stones. Then we'd skidaddle down along the back of the tenement houses out to a small alleyway. When I got home and my mother found out what I had done - I got a beating."

But there was more trouble to come.

"They had wire-cages on the trucks to protect themselves, so we couldn't see how many were inside," Kevin recalled. "One night we were there ready to make our attack again, but we didn't realise some of them had gotten out already further up the hill. We trashed them with stones and ran away down the alleyway - and they were there waiting for us. We got a beating from them. When I got home and told what had happened - my mother gave me another beating!"

How the Duffys and Dowdalls Teamed Up

The Civil War in Ireland ended in 1923, with Michael Collins assassinated and de Valera beginning his slow return to power and his overseeing of the Irish Free State's evolution into the Republic of Ireland. Barney was a lifetime supporter of de Valera and the Fianna Fail party Dev would eventually form to get back into the mainstream of Ireland's politics.

Barney's brother Kevin remembered how his mother made delicious cakes. She would leave them out on the windowsill to cool off, and that would be his chance to sneak up and steal one. This could hardly have happened in Brabazon Street - where they lived on the top floor - but then he also had many memories of being in Cork - and of one time swimming out from Cobh to Spike Island - so the family spent time out of the city. Barney's brother Peter was also a powerful swimmer, and was known to go on long swims out to sea.

One day, Barney's mother Ellen was standing on a chair on a table to hang curtains and her young son John came along and tickled her on the back of the leg as a joke. She fell and suffered a severe injury to her back - in the family, it was said that she broke her back. Thereafter, Ellen walked with a very extreme stoop and was in constant pain. She did not tell the truth about how the accident happened to her husband until she was on her death bed.

When Patrick Ambrose Duffy settled to live in Dublin, he got a garden allotment in Rathmines which he nurtured with great care and skill. The plot had a long wall against which he built two greenhouses. He grew all kinds of vegetables, but also pear trees and grapes and tomatoes - none of which his children were allowed to touch.

"There was a Kerry Blue dog that my father kept in the garden as a guard dog," Kevin recalled. "One time, John and I went to the garden and climbed over the gate - planning on taking some fruit - and by God! John thought he could pacify the dog but it grabbed him!"

Kevin remembered that "If John - my next older brother - and I ever did anything wrong, our punishment was that we had to do the weeding in the garden. There was part of the plot that always had white turnips in it, and John and I had to get down on our hands and knees and weed them.

"But our father was a lovely man," Kevin added with a laugh.

There was another side to Patrick Ambrose. Kevin remembered that his father would often take his two youngest sons for a tram ride around Dublin on Sundays. This ride usually ended at a pub, with the boys sitting outside while their father had a drink inside.

"I remember one time John and I were sitting outside," Kevin recalled, "when suddenly - bang! - a man came flying out the door. Moments later the barman came out with our lemonade. 'what was that about?' we asked him. 'That was your father,' he said. My father loved animals, but in the pub he had accidentally stood on a dog's tail. My father was very tall, and someone had said to him 'you're so tall, you'd stand on it if it was on the ceiling'. Father walloped him."

And now to Molly and her family background. The Dowdall clan is not Irish. They were established in

How the Duffys and Dowdalls Teamed Up

Ireland not long after the Anglo-Norman invasion and are to be found mostly in 'the Pale' - the British stronghold of Dublin and Louth. The clan comes from the Yorkshire region of Britain and its name comes from an English place-name: Dovedale. This was later gaelicised to Dowdall. There is a Dowdallstown in County Louth. Given Molly's father's name, it's also worth noting that a Luke Dowdall was Lord Mayor of Dublin in 1413-14, and that in the late 17th century there was a Sir Luke Dowdall and a Captain Luke Dowdall in Dublin.

Molly's parents were both from Donnycarney, a suburb on the Northside of Dublin. Her mother's name was Elizabeth Farrell (coincidentally, Molly's mother and Barney's mother had the same maiden name) and she was born on January 1st 1882 in County Dublin. Molly's father's name was Luke Dowdall. Both Luke and Elizabeth were teetotallers. There are some indications that both came from at least comfortable backgrounds and that possibly Luke's parents owned a shop.

Luke had no sisters. His brothers were James, Benny, Barkel, Willie, and Gary. Benny and Barkel emigrated to America. James emigrated to Australia. One of Luke Dowdall's brothers, Benny, would return to Dublin and this story decades later. James maintained occasional contact. The rest disappear from the story - although Barkel would crop up decades later to add a slight complication to the life of one of Barney and Molly's children.

Molly's mother Elizabeth had sisters but no brothers. One sister was Margaret, who Molly believed lived to be over 100 years old. Another sister, Mary (later Mary Byrd) was a piano teacher and is said to have received a university education in music. Mary lived in Summerhill Parade, and gave lessons there. Many years later her daughter, named Lily, got a degree in music too and became a teacher. They ultimately moved to Belton Park Avenue in Donnycarney. Only Molly's Aunt Mary crops up again in this story.

The gift of music was on both sides of the family. Luke Dowdall's brother Gary had a daughter, Mary, who became a popular singer and appeared often at the Royal Theatre in Dublin and a son, Terry, who was a pianist. The gift may go a long way back. Brian Boydell, professor of music in Trinity College, wrote a history of Irish music in which is mentioned a Spackling (a nickname for Francis) Dowdall in the 18th century. He had the distinction of being thrown out of the state orchestra in 1723 for 'misbehaviour' - although the offence was not described.

Molly was born when the family lived on Church Street, off the North Wall, on Friday April 12th 1907: a healthy baby with bright blue eyes. She was christened Mary Josephine Anne - named exactly after her mother's mother. Molly was the eldest, and after her came the twins Maggie and Lily, then Luke, Delia and Willie.

"I remember my Mammy having four of us in a pram, walking up along East Wall Road," Molly said.

Molly also remembered some of her uncles.

"I remember Barkel was a real gentleman and had a walking stick," Molly said. "He was very skinny and looked a lot like his brother Willie - but Willie drank like a fish. Willie was the youngest."

Molly's parents were always known as 'Mother Dowdall' and 'Father Dowdall' to Barney and Molly's children, and that is how they will be referred to for the rest of the book. Molly's father worked for Merchants Warehousing in East Wall, and the family got one of the workers' cottages on East Road. They lived there in the years of Molly's early childhood, although for some reason they were constantly moving home. Molly recalled that they lived in Clontarf, in a flat in Vernon Avenue. She went to school on the Malahide Road at that time. They finally moved to Buckingham Street in Summerhill, in the centre of Dublin City's Northside, and then Molly went to Rutland Street School.

It is said that Molly's father once saved a child's life on East Wall Road, and this turned out to be the child of one of the bosses of Merchant Warehousing who guaranteed him his job for life. Many years later, something would come to light that added great credibility to this story.

Although he did indeed work all his life for Merchant Warehousing, Molly said that her father had owned a business at some stage too.

Father Dowdall always smoked a pipe. He did so even during his work - which he was not supposed to do. He told of times when a foreman would approach him and he would pocket his pipe. The foreman would deliberately stay talking with him for a long while - expecting smoke to start rising from the coat pocket. This would never happen, because Father Dowdall's pipe had a small lid that he could flick over it. The man was a cardiac asthmatic, however, and his smoking would ultimately cost him his life.

"We were quare kids," Molly said. "We wouldn't be let play with everybody, and when we weren't let play then the other kids would come along and pull the hair off you, and then our mother would come down, and then there'd be a row and you'd be kept in."

Her father could be very strict. She recalled how once her mother called her to come in but she was waiting beside an ice cream van and had answered "I'll come in a minute." Her father came racing out and chased her around the ice cream van. Molly ran into the house and hid under a bed. Her father dragged her out from under the bed with a sweeping brush and beat her for being bold.

"My father was very hard if anything went wrong," she said. "He wanted you to grow up to be a lady and always keep your head up."

She had her chores. One was to go down to Kennedy's Bakery to buy a shilling's worth of broken bread. "there would be buns and everything in it."

It was a hard life and a constant struggle. "There was times when we had our tea and times when we hadn't. My mother and father would give it to us and did without themselves, and then when there would be a bit of grub in the house we'd all sit down to it," Molly said.

Molly was often up to mischief. "I got more hidings than the others," she recalled. "I got hidings for looking crooked." Mind you, looking cross-eyed - or 'gunner-eyed', as she called it - was an ambition she had at one stage. She said she would sit for hours with her eyes crossed and get her friend to thump her on the back because she had heard that if you got a shock you could be left cross-eyed. Years later, precisely that would happen to one of her children.

"I got in trouble in school too," she said. "I used to call the teacher Bull-eyed Briscoe. My mother was called up to the school I don't know how many times."

How the Duffys and Dowdalls Teamed Up

The Dowdalls usually went to Mass at the pro-cathedral in Marlborough Street. "It wasn't just that you went to Mass," Molly said, "you had to be seen to be going to Mass." Molly and her sisters Maggie and Lily made their confirmation on the same day in the pro-cathedral - the three of them dressed the same.

In those days, there was no custom of visiting family or neighbours after the confirmation. "We just played out on the street in our dresses and people passing by might give you a couple of pence."

Molly had an adventure when she was young that had a big impact on her.

"One day I went out on the boat to Lambay Island with my pal May Redmond," she recalled. "She told me that if I smoked a cigarette I wouldn't feel seasick. So I did - and I never will forget it. I was getting sick every day for a month. My father and mother were killing me over it. But I never smoked again."

Molly was wilful and disobedient; the mischievous girl became a spirited young woman. She was notorious for sneaking out without her parents knowing, or for staying out late. One time, her father discovered that she was seeing a boyfriend. He was furious. Her father tied Molly to the foot of the bed, then brought the young man in and showed him how Molly was being punished. The boyfriend never showed up again.

Father Dowdall didn't believe that women should work, and so when Molly left school she was at home helping her mother every day. This certainly didn't suit Molly. In those days, there was a tradition of making lunch for the men and bringing it to them at lunchtime. Molly volunteered for this task - it was her way of getting out and flirting with the boys.

Miss Mary Dowdall

The story of Barney and Molly is peppered with some events that seem hard to believe. One tall tale from Molly's youth is about the time her mother bought a piano for sixpence. Mother Dowdall was walking past a music instrument shop on Henry Street and saw the 'sixpence' price tag on the piano and went in to buy it. The salesman explained that the price tag had fallen off something else onto the piano and this was not its true price. She insisted, threatening to call in the police, and the salesman relented.

Can that be true? Who knows. Mother Dowdall was certainly imposing enough to get away with such a coup.

The Dublin that Barney and Molly were growing up in was poor, battered, disease-ridden and dangerous. It was the capital of a poverty stricken country. It had the highest death rate in the British Isles, the unemployment figure was 20% and unskilled workers in Ireland earned up to a third less than those in the rest of the British Isles.

From the beginning of the 19th century, the wealthy English had left their grand city homes and returned to England. Houses worth 8,000 pounds in those times were being sold off for as little as 500 pounds to landlords who then rented out the rooms to families. Up to a hundred people lived in a tenement house, with families of up to fifteen living in a room - such houses having one toilet and one water tap in the yard to serve all its tenants. The Great Famine of the mid 19th century had, through death and emigration, halved the population of Ireland: yet the population of Dublin rose as desperate, homeless people came to the capital city hoping to find work and shelter. Dublin was considered to have the worst slums in Europe, and Dublin had the highest infant mortality rate and general death rate of any city in the United Kingdom.

What's more, the landlords were free to evict anyone at any time for any - or no - reason. No laws existed for the protection or welfare of people living in tenements. Yet a third of Dubliners lived in them, and all the records tell that there was a great sense of community and friendship among the people of Dublin's inner city. So it was when Barney Duffy and Molly Dowdall met on the streets of their hometown.

When all those people gathered in 1987 to celebrate the 80th birthday of the woman who had given birth to their clan, they might have paused to raise a toast in honour of a bicycle. Molly was cycling along Portland Row in Summerhill, passing by what was then the

School for the Blind, when she fell off her bike. Barney was walking by at the time and went to her help. Molly was sixteen years old when she first met Barney. He was twenty. This was around the time of the end of the Irish Civil War and it was the start of their romance.

Barney worked in Moylan's public house in Summerhill, and Molly had noticed him around the area. She was the one who made the first moves - who knows even if the bicycle fall was really an accident.

A problem for Molly - who never drank and was the child of parents who never drank - was that Barney was very fond of the drink. One of his jobs in Moylan's pub was to fill the porter bottles down in the cellar of the pub.

"He'd pour 'a sup for you and a sup for me' when he was doing the bottles," Molly said. "That's the way it was with him. Barney used to drink like a trooper. One night he was going home and had a bottle of whiskey in his jacket. He fell getting on the bus and smashed it. His stomach was so badly cut he had to go to hospital."

When Barney met Molly's parents, they were unimpressed. They didn't feel he was up to the standard they expected for their daughter. Molly's mother, an austere woman, had probably hoped her daughter would find a young man with a trade or with better prospects.

Molly met Barney's family. Barney and his brothers and sister adored their mother, Ellen. Molly said Ellen was a very beautiful woman, and remembered how, when she visited their home in Brabazon Street, Ellen would always be wearing a white apron and have a white cloth on the table. Ellen was very elegant, and she usually wore tops with the high-neck Victorian collars and kept her hair tied back in a bun. The Duffys were a handsome family - when Barney stepped out with his brothers Peter and Paddy and their father, many heads would turn.

Ellen Duffy said to Molly "please take care of my Barney." He was the frail one in the family, always thin and delicate. He had always had problems with his stomach. Molly developed a great affection for Ellen.

Dancing was the greatest joy in Molly's life. "We'd get together in the middle of the road. Someone would start playing a mouth organ or a tin whistle and the dancing would start. We'd dance until midnight. The next day would be the same - people came in from work and had something to eat, then they'd meet again out on the street and the music and dancing would begin again."

There was a crossroads at Ballybough that was the most popular meeting place. Such a sight would have brought delight to Barney's hero de Valera, who would speak of his vision of Ireland as a place with 'comely maidens dancing at the crossroads'. In 1926, as Barney and Molly's romance was leading to the altar, de Valera founded a new political party - Fianna Fail; the soldiers of destiny. The party dedicated itself to the vision of a united independent Ireland with its own living language and culture. It was a tall order for a little island. In the same year, Ireland also established its own radio station - launched as 2RN.

Barney and Molly, meanwhile, would go to their nights of dancing and then get the last bus home. She would get off at Summerhill and he would carry on to his home in Brabazon Street. Molly recalled how she would arrive into the unlit tenement and make her way up the stairs and was usually met by a rat somewhere along the way. It was not unusual, too, to see homeless people sleeping on the landings of the stairs.

Barney and Molly were in love, and in the years of their courtship they accepted the hardships that lay in store for a young couple such as them in impoverished Ireland. There is a photograph of Molly that survives from before her married years. It is a studio photograph of 'Miss Dowdall' showing Molly probably around the time of her eighteenth birthday. She is wearing a ring on her wedding finger that must be her engagement ring. Her dark hair is beautifully styled and she looks very elegant in pose and dress. This was Barney's bride-to-be: the woman who would ultimately raise thirteen children as she and her husband shared their lives and struggles.

"You only marry the one you want," Molly said. "Even if they never worked. It's not money that will make you happy. If you like the person, you'll be happy. To the day Barney died I never wanted for a cut of bread."

Barney and Molly were married on 18th July 1926. Molly had just turned 19. It was the day before Barney's 23rd birthday. They had been courting for almost three years.

The wedding took place in Our Lady of Lourdes church on Gloucester Street.

"We'd a wedding for a week," Molly remembered. "We got married on a Saturday, and the party went on until the following Saturday."

A lifelong friend of Barney's, Georgie Brennan, made the cakes for them. "We had so much food, we ended up giving it away," Molly said.

How the Duffys and Dowdalls Teamed Up

Barney and Molly had their honeymoon in Bray, County Wicklow, a holiday town along the Dublin south coast.

Sadly, there is no photograph of the newlyweds. But events a few months later gave what was probably the reason for no photographs being passed down for posterity.

A Young Family in Dublin's Inner City

The marriage of Barney and Molly got off to a very difficult start. On November 5th, four months after the wedding, Barney's mother Ellen died at the age of forty nine. The death certificate shows that she died in the Hospice for the Dying in Harold's Cross. The cause of death was 'generalised tuberculosis and cardiac failure'. This left Patrick Ambrose Duffy widowed for the second time: now with thirteen year old Kevin and fourteen year old John at home.

Later the same month, Molly gave birth to a daughter in the Rotunda Hospital. Barney and Molly named the child Ellen. Their address on the birth certificate is 41, Summerhill. This child died two months later on February 1st 1927. The cause of death is stated as 'convulsions and cardiac failure' - the baby had taken a seizure and died. By then Barney and Molly were living with Molly's parents, as their address is 8, Casino Road. The certificate also states that Barney witnessed and reported the death.

It must have been a terrible blow to the couple. For Barney, he had lost his mother and his first child in the space of two months. The child mortality rate in the Dublin tenements was five times the rate in the rest of the country: more than one in ten children died before the age of one year. This could not have dulled the pain for the young couple, but it was the terrible reality of the time.

Around then, Barney decided to change job. "He was drinking too much," Molly said, "and he knew he had to either give up the job or it would be the end of him."

Molly, for the one and only time in her life, got a job. She was hired as a housemaid. Her father would never have allowed it when she was single, but now it would be an attempt by the young couple to save some money for themselves.

A reference survives from March 1927 from a Mrs Frederick Kennedy of Scribblestown House, Castleknock, County Dublin. It states; 'I wish to recommend Bernard Duffy who is an experienced young gardener. Very hard working, strictly honest, sober and quiet. Also his wife whom I am sure will give satisfaction in any work they may undertake as they are most respectable young people.'

Later the same year, Barney had a reference from MM Loftus, Pea Packers and Fruit Importers, of Rutland Street. This reference, signed by M. Loftus, may have been written as a favour, because it states 'We have known Mister Duffy for the past five or six years, during which time we have always found him very respectable, honest, and obliging. We can thoroughly recommend him for any position that may be given him.'

On January 28th 1928 Molly gave birth to another girl, and she was named Elizabeth - Betty - after Molly's mother. Betty was born in the Rotunda Hospital, but Molly had most of her following children at home.

The arrangement of living with Molly's parents didn't last very long, because when the children started coming there was not enough room.

The family moved to a flat in Rutland Place. It was a three-roomed flat and the rent was three shillings a week. They lived over a butcher shop, Kavanaghs. Molly was moving back in around the area of her childhood - back to tenement life with its famous sense of community and its infamous hardships.

"It was very difficult to find a place to live in Dublin then," Molly said.

Around this time, Molly started going out on dates with a man named Paddy Slevin. Molly's mother would mind Betty so that Molly could go out with him. Barney's father saw Molly and Paddy going off together from time to time. "All he'd do was shake his fist," Molly said. The reason for this pretty unconventional situation was dancing. Molly loved dancing, and Barney didn't dance.

"Many's the time I danced down in Ballybough with all the girls and fellas," Molly said, "but I still didn't want anyone but Barney."

Barney worked with his father doing gardens. This didn't earn enough money and he sought other work. As with the vast majority of men at the time, however, he could find no permanent work and hunted instead for any form of available casual work.

"He never sat home five minutes," Molly said. "Anywhere he could earn a shilling, he'd be gone. People knew him and would come to the door asking for him to do odd jobs and he'd be off on his bicycle first thing in the morning." But Barney's search for work was not always successful and the couple sometimes needed help.

There was a man named Gogan, from Finglas, who was the Relieving Officer. He would go around people's homes to examine the need they were in.

"If he smelt that anything was frying," Molly said, "he'd ask you where did you get it and how did you buy it. One time, this man was informed by someone that Barney was being seen going out at the same time early every morning - even though at that time we were getting help because he was unemployed. This Grogan came one morning early looking for Barney and I said he'd be back in a minute. The man sat at the door waiting. Lucky enough, it turned out there was no work for Barney that day in the place he had gone to so he came back."

One time, the struggle to survive was so difficult that a man from St Vincent de Paul came to see them. He noticed there was bread and butter on the table.

"What kind of butter is that," he asked her.

"Ordinary butter," Molly replied.

"Then we can't give you any help. If you can put butter instead of margarine on the table you don't need help."

This was the time of the American 'Great Depression' - the effects of which were felt all over the world. In 1929, none of the adult Duffy brothers had work.

Barney's brother Kevin recalled a time when Patrick Ambrose went to his three older sons and said 'go to my allotment and sell everything from it' and so the men went to work clearing it out. They sold everything that was growing there, and it kept them going for about three months - which shows how big and well kept the garden was.

"I remember one day going to see my brothers and they were weighing out potatoes in a bag," Kevin said. "They didn't have a scales."

On September 14th the same year, Molly gave birth to a baby boy whom they named Bernard. The child was born at home in yet another new address - 11 Brabazon Street.

The move from Summerhill to the flat on the top floor of 11, Brabazon Street, off the Coombe, was of mutual benefit to them and Barney's father - but an increase in Molly's workload. They shared the flat with Patrick Ambrose Duffy, who was living with his sons Paddy, John and Kevin and daughter Nellie. Patrick Ambrose's daughter from his first marriage, Maggie, no longer lived at home.

"Nellie wasn't cooking for them and they had to get up and do their own cooking and washing," Molly said, "so Mister Duffy asked me and Barney if we'd go over. We got the big room."

When Barney and Molly moved in, Molly took over much of the domestic work and became a kind of foster mother for the younger children. The flat consisted of one large living room and another long room that was used as the bedroom for Molly and Barney and their children. Typical of living conditions at the time, they had an oil lamp or gas for light and they cooked on the open fire. There was, of course, no refrigeration and accounts of the time say that flies were a constant problem, spreading disease.

A doubtful convenience for Molly was the fact that they lived around the corner from Dublin's main maternity hospital, the Coombe Hospital. That said, Molly also told how in those days it was considered crude to show that you were pregnant. If someone came to visit, it was typical for a pregnant woman to sit at the table to hide her belly.

There was a rule against having dogs in the Brabazon Street building, but Barney's brother Paddy kept one hidden. He had a routine of taking the dog out in the evenings when his father had gone asleep, and then hiding the dog above them in the attic. Molly recalled that one night, in the middle of the night as all were sleeping, the dog fell out of the attic and landed on top of Mister Duffy. "The man nearly died of a heart attack," Molly joked.

The sleeping arrangements were not the most comfortable. The base was too small for the mattress Paddy and Mister Duffy slept on, and the bed often collapsed under them, sending them rolling onto the floor.

Paddy was very strong and athletic. He was two years younger than Barney.

"He had a shirt as black as the fire grate," Molly remembered. "The collar and cuffs would be lovely and white, and he wore a dickey-front. But the shirt would be black. Sometimes, he'd come home dressed up like this and he'd be at the table and one of us would sneak around and pull out the dickey-front and there would be the shirt. I never saw a shirt as dirty in my life."

Paddy married Maggie Mulvaney. They were ballroom dancers.

Barney and Molly hit a very tragic time in 1930. Barney, never a robust man, was taken in to what was then known as the fever hospital on Cork Street. He was grievously ill and it was not known if he would live. At the time, diphtheria and tuberculosis (known then as 'consumption') were very common in the tenements.

While Barney was in hospital, their son Bernard was struck with gastritis and was taken in to the same hospital. It is said that a priest told Molly "pray for which one you want to live. Both lives are at risk, and you can't have both." Whatever about that wisdom, the view at the time would have been to save the father and take the child.

The story of what happened next is as incredible as it is tragic, but all are convinced it is true. A nurse had decided that some form of sun lamp treatment might help the child Bernard and he was placed under this. The nurse, however, forgot about him and he suffered fatal burns. The child died soon after. Molly was informed of the death when she went to the hospital - and then had to go visit her weak and possibly mortally ill husband.

"You know," he said to Molly, "I kept thinking I heard our Bernard crying and screaming here yesterday."

Molly assured him it was his imagination - that Bernard and Betty were at home safe and well. She chose not to risk telling him the truth when he was in such a weak state.

The death certificate for Bernard, showing that he died on April 7th 1930, gave the cause of death as gastritis - from which he had been suffering for four months - and showed that the six month old child indeed died in Cork Street Hospital.

Then came what is probably the most extraordinary episode in the couple's life. Coming home from visiting her husband one evening, and now having buried their baby son, Molly was climbing the stairs of the Brabazon Street flat when she found a newborn baby wrapped up, abandoned, in a basket. Molly took the baby in. It was a girl and the mother, for whatever reasons of desperation, had left the child there.

Molly started caring for the child as if it were her own. In a further bizarre twist to the story, she started finding small items for the baby - food or clothes - left outside the door of her flat. The mother knew that Molly had her baby and was leaving things there for her child.

This situation carried on for several weeks until Barney, recovered from his illness, came home. He was confronted with the tragic discovery that his son had died, and he saw his wife with a child he knew was not their own. Molly wanted to keep the child but Barney refused. He called the police, who took the baby away and started their investigation to find the mother. No one knows if the mother was found or what happened to the girl. Molly and Barney had now lost two of their first three children. They got on with their lives, dealing with their grief as best they could. Those were the cruelest and hardest of times.

On September 25th 1931, Molly gave birth to another daughter. This child, who was named Maureen, was born with what is known as the 'caul'. This is a portion of the membrane that encloses the foetus which sometimes envelopes the head of a child at birth. It's regarded as lucky and is said to mean the person with it will never drown. For that reason, it is valued by sailors - who would buy them.

With Barney and Molly's family growing, Barney's father left the shared flat and moved just a few houses down the road on the opposite side to a flat of his own. It was on the top floor above a corner shop. Molly and Barney then used the living room also as their bedroom, and the other room as the bedroom for their children.

Patrick Ambrose Duffy was very fond of Barney and Molly's children. He would often take his little granddaughter Betty off to the pub and she would sit in the porch as he was inside having his drink.

"There used to be little packets of biscuits," Betty remembered, "and he'd bring me out one of those and a glass of minerals and I'd sit there and wait until he'd had his drink."

Then he would come out and lift her onto his shoulders and carry her home.

"He was a lovely, gorgeous man," Betty said.

"He was a very jolly man," Maureen recalled. "I can still picture him, standing at the fire, twiddling his moustache."

Barney's youngest brother, Kevin, had completed his apprenticeship in Kavanagh's grocery store on the Coombe, but he wanted a more adventurous career.

He applied to join the Royal Irish Guards, but when he went to London for his medical it was found that he fell half an inch short of the required height - he needed to be at least 5 foot 10 inches.

"One of the only regiments open for recruiting then was the Suffolk Regiment," Kevin recalled. "I met an old boy in London, Bert Hughes - he was an engineer and he'd gone broke - and we decided to join the Suffolk Regiment. We went to Whitehall - a big recruiting centre - and joined."

Patrick Ambrose Duffy worked for Sir George Murphy - a man whose business had something to do with coal and oil. He designed the garden for the Murphy home on Shrewsbury Road in Ballsbridge, near Lansdowne Road railway station, making a lawn and a rose garden with a sun dial.

One day, his employer asked Patrick Ambrose to clean the family's cars. He refused.

"No, I'm a gardener," he told his boss. Instead, his son Paddy - who was a motor mechanic - was hired to clean and maintain the cars.

It was when working for the Murphys that Patrick Ambrose met the parlour maid, Margaret Lennox - known as Peg - and began courting her. She was almost thirty years his junior. They had already been working together for some years, and she addressed him as 'Pat'.

He was a very charming man. When he was wooing his third wife-to-be, he would put a rose in the lapel of his jacket and another in the band of his hat - and this he would give to her when they met.

"He was very gentle," she recalled. "and he had a grand manner. He'd walk out of a room before he'd have a row.

"Every day, I would bring him his lunch," she recalled. "I had to always bring him a full box of matches for his pipe, because he'd work and forget about the pipe and then he'd have to light it again."

Barney also said his father was very forgetful. Barney remembered times when his father would go around the house looking for his hat - with the hat on his head.

"He wore a hard hat on Sundays," Peg Duffy recalled, "and a soft hat on the weekdays when working."

Mister Duffy was very conscious of his appearance and also liked to receive a complement if, for instance, he had bought a new shirt. Realising this, his sons used to deliberately pretend they hadn't noticed. If he nudged them by saying 'do you notice anything different', each would give a different wrong answer.

"We would visit Barney and Molly. The children were told to call me Miss Lennox," Mrs Peg Duffy recalled with a laugh.

Peg had a spinster aunt, Mary, who was against the idea of the couple marrying.

"She told me I should find a younger man, instead of marrying an old widower," Peg said. "On that account, I didn't run after him, you know. But no matter where I went he found me. Someone told him I went to Donnybrook Church, and he was standing outside the church one morning waiting for me. Another time, he had sent me a postcard with a big red rose."

They were married in 1932. Patrick Ambrose and his new bride lived in the lodge of Lansdowne House, just beside the Lansdowne Road railway station.

This was the year the 31st Eucharistic Congress was held in Dublin in June. One day, 200,000 men attended a Mass in Phoenix Park. The following day, 200,000 women attended a Mass for women. Two days later, almost a million people attended a Pontifical Mass in Phoenix Park.

On November 7th of this year, Molly gave birth to another girl. This child was named Bernadette but would always be known as Breda.

By 1933, de Valera and his Fianna Fail party were in government and he continued to buck against lingering British control. The Irish government was obliged to pay annual compensation of four million pounds to Britain for loss of income caused through the country's independence and Dev refused to continue making these payments. An Economic War broke out between Ireland and England and yet again it was a struggle for ordinary people to find work and to survive. This battle between the two countries would go on until 1938, ending with victory for Dev's strategies and a kind of economic independence for the twenty six county Irish Free State.

Patrick Ambrose was enjoying his new married life and new home. He was also going to become a father again. Mrs Peg Duffy recalled a time when she was pregnant and her new husband's sister made a visit to Dublin for a week. Peg and Patrick Ambrose slept on the couch in the livingroom to give the visitors the bedroom.

"He told me she was a dressmaker in the main street in Monaghan," she recalled. "She had a daughter with her."

Late in 1933, Peg gave birth to their son who was christened Ambrose. It must have been a time of celebration between Barney and his father - the former now with three children and a pregnant wife, the latter having a new lease of life as husband and father. In February the following year, however, tragedy struck.

"One time," Kevin said, "my brothers Peter, Barney and Paddy called around to our father and said 'come on, let's go for a drink'. He refused, and said he hadn't been drinking. He was dead within forty eight hours." If the timing is so, it is quite possible that the brothers had called around to celebrate the fact that Molly had given birth to a baby son, Luke, on February 11th 1934.

Luke and Amby

Kevin's view that the marriage led to his father's death is one that was prevalent in the family. Many in the family said that Mister Duffy died 'of a knot in his stomach because his wife wouldn't let him drink'.

Peg Duffy said that her husband died of peritonitis - a burst appendix - but his death certificate shows a surprising grain of truth in the family legend. The events of his last days explain how this is so.

Patrick Ambrose was immensely proud of his new born son. He would take a stroll with his wife and child, and he would push the pram. One day in mid February, however, they were walking along and he asked Peg to push the pram. He then also took off his coat and laid it across the pram. It was the first indication that something was wrong.

Later that day at home, he was in increasing pain. The next day, he was taken into Sir Patrick Dun's Hospital.

He was found to have intussusception toxaemia. This is a telescoping of the intestine, whereby one piece of intestine folds in to another piece - it can also occur at the appendix. The condition causes the blood supply to the folded part of intestine to be cut off, killing the tissue. It also causes intestinal contents to build up behind the point of intussusception, putting pressure on the folded piece of gut, further cutting off the blood supply. The intestine then ruptures, releasing the intestinal contents into the abdominal cavity, which causes an overwhelming - and in those days fatal - infection. He was operated on, but to no avail. He died in hospital on February 16th. Patrick Ambrose was fifty seven years old.

He had died of a knot in his stomach.

His son Ambrose was only four months old when Patrick Ambrose died. It is ironic that this man who had become a father again late in his life died of a condition that is extremely rare in adulthood and most common in early childhood.

Betty remembered going up to see her grandfather's remains in the hospital.

"I loved him," she said. "As young as I was, I remember seeing him and kissing him."

He was laid to rest in the grave of his second wife, Ellen, in Mount Jerome cemetery.

"Mrs Duffy didn't like him drinking," Betty said, "and I know it caused terrible resentment when he died. His family wouldn't give her the burial papers, so that she could not be buried with her husband."

Patrick Ambrose's eldest daughter, Maggie, referred to Peg Duffy as 'the woman who killed the old man'. Barney held no such view or grudge. He and Molly would be a constant support to Peg Duffy: a widow raising a child alone. As Barney and Molly's children grew - and as more children came along - there was a slight puzzle as to how they should address Peg Duffy. She wasn't their aunt. She wasn't their grandmother. In the end, just as Molly's parents would be known as 'Father Dowdall' and 'Mother Dowdall', Peg Duffy would be known as 'Old Mrs Duffy'. Barney used to call his brother 'young Amby'.

At the time of his father's death, Kevin, at his army barracks in Britain, was given the news and offered the choice of going back to Ireland. Kevin realised that by the time he got to Dublin the funeral would be over and so he declined the offer. Kevin would never set foot in Ireland again, and he would never see his brother

Barney again. The latter is the source of another story that would not resurface for almost forty years.

Kevin Tammany Duffy

Most of the brothers became scattered in the years to come. Peter lived with his wife Mary in Irishtown, while Paddy remained in the inner city. Later, a daughter of his, Margaret, would become a trader selling vegetables on Moore Street.

"John was very good to me when his father died," Peg Duffy recalled. "He used to come around and see Amby. A job of his in the army was to bring up the horses for the Horse Show, and he'd drop in and see me." John, later in life, moved to London. He was dubbed 'John the Liar' by Barney. "He'd tell you one thing today and it'd be different the next day." John ended up living in Kilburn in London. He is also said to have married several times - usually to much older women.

Barney and Molly

Eight years into their marriage, Barney and Molly had endured much on top of the hardships faced by all working class people in Dublin at that time. Barney had lost both his parents, he had been in hospital close to death, and the couple had lost two of their first six children. A favourite expression Molly always had was 'there's a good day coming', and such a day must have seemed very far off for them in their tenement in the Coombe.

'Old Mrs Duffy' told an intriguing story. She said that her late husband had discovered a cure for potato blight. This cure had already passed two levels of testing, with just one more to go, when he died. It would, she said, have made a huge amount of money for him.

"He was already planning the house we were going to buy," she said, "and a big plot of land in Nutfield." That being so, if Barney's father had lived and acquired such property and wealth, then the years of struggle and hardship lying ahead for Barney and Molly would never have happened. Could it all have been lost for the lack of a few pints of Guinness?

11 Brabazon Street

The family had a new addition on June 17th 1935 when Molly gave birth to another daughter, whom they named Margaret - known as Greta. Much later this prompted the nickname 'Garbo'. While Barney was out struggling to find enough work, Molly was at home raising five children under the age of seven.

The tenement area was getting ever more run down and there was constant public outcry about the fact that the new Irish government wasn't doing enough to save the people living in these parts of Dublin. Electricity, already long having made its way through Dublin and its suburbs and extended beyond, had not yet reached Brabazon Street where the homes were still lit by gaslight and food was still being cooked on opens fires.

"To all intents and purposes, the houses were derelict," Luke recalled. "They were dumps in a state of collapse and just waiting to be pulled down."

The most feared danger to life and health was the huge population of rats.

"The place was alive with rats," Molly said. "They bit Luke on the nose, and Betty was bitten twice." Other writings about the Liberties in those days tell some horrific stories concerning rats. They would be attracted by the smell of food - which was what would lead them to bite children. But there were even stories of women with newborn babies waking to find rats on their breasts, drawn by the smell of the milk.

"The rats used to run over us in the bed," Betty recalled. "We all got fever one time - the landlord had put down poison, and all the rats died under the floorboards and rotted. They took up the floorboards - and there was a mass of dead rats."

Luke recalled a time when a huge rat was trapped in the bowl of the communal toilet and his Uncle Paddy was the one who reached in to drag it out and kill it.

"The usual thing was that you'd hear a scream and then you'd know someone had come across a rat in the toilet again," he said. "Usually, two of the brothers would go down and try in each side of the toilet - each one hoping that they weren't going to be reaching in for the head end of the rat." He remembers also a time when a huge rat had been caught in a cage and the gruesomely difficult time the men had trying to kill it.

"When I was small, I remember Mam making the fire," Maureen said. "While we were having breakfast and getting ready for school, she'd be lighting the fire. I remember one time Mam asked Betty to get her a bundle of sticks. Betty got the sticks and just threw them beside her. 'I'm getting ready for school,' Betty said. 'If you want something, there's others in the room'. Mam took up the bundle of sticks and threw them at her."

Molly was often stressed by the pressures of children and housework and could be short tempered.

"She'd hit you with whatever she had in her hand," Betty recalled, saying that she carried a scar on her shoulder and another on her leg from different incidents. She also told one story that turned out unexpectedly. Molly loved music and she had a gramophone player and had a collection of 78rpm records. "Someone had bought Mammy a new record and it was her favourite. I had done something to annoy her and she shouted 'I'll kill ya!' She hit me - but what did she have in her hand? Her new record. It didn't hurt me, but it fell to pieces. She nearly went mad."

Betty also admitted of herself that she was 'wild'. She was known as a tomboy, and was constantly getting into trouble. In fact, Betty seems to have been very much like Molly as a child.

Molly was obviously overwhelmed by the housework, and Betty remembered her taking some extreme actions.

"Mammy used to tie us around the waist to the kitchen chairs so that we wouldn't dirty the house," she said. "And dare you move." If Molly had to do something that would mean having to leave the children alone - such as going down the flights of stairs to fetch water - she would tie them to the chairs to make sure they couldn't, for instance, go near the fireplace or harm themselves.

Once, when Betty was put in charge of minding her small sisters and brother, she took them out to Stephen's Green. Maureen climbed on spiked railings and slipped, cutting herself. Betty took her to hospital and Maureen was fine - but Betty walked the streets for hours afterwards with the children because she was afraid of what Molly would do when she saw Maureen bandaged.

Betty, being the oldest, was also the first to be handed on house chores.

"I used to have to scrub the stairs in the house," Betty said. "There were two flights that we had to keep clean. There was a woman named Mrs Kelly who lived on the same floor as us, and she would do the stairs one week and we'd do it the next. I remember times when I'd be scrubbing the stairs, and Daddy would come along and see me there and he'd whisper 'Come on and we'll go off to the pictures' and he'd bring me to the Royal or the Gaiety. Or he might buy me something - a cheap bracelet - and he'd say 'there - that's for doing the stairs'. He was the one who made me feel great."

Betty recalled a time in Brabazon Street when Barney taught her how to skate. "In the house where we lived there was a big long hall, and he taught me how to skate in the hall. After that I was a brilliant skater - up and down Brabazon Street. We kids used to have competitions."

Around that time, Barney would go to an area called Carman's Hall off Christchurch to play cards. "If he was lucky and he won," Betty said, "he used to come back with a bag of sweets."

Molly and Barney loved listening to radio - she for the music and he for the news. A vivid memory for Luke was the job of going down to a shop on the corner of The Coombe and Meath Street with the large, rechargeable battery for a replacement.

"I remember going down the stairs and down the 150 yards or so to the corner shop," he said. "They were big acid batteries with handles, and I'd walk along swinging the battery by the handle. It's a miracle I never burned myself with the acid."

Luke went to school in Frances Street, and he had a teacher named Mrs McCaffrey.

"I got a couple of good hidings from her," he remembered. "One time, she had stepped up on a desk to close a window and I said to the boy beside me

11 Brabazon Street

'wouldn't it be great fun if she fell out' and she heard me. I got a clatter for that." Her family had a shop on Patrick Street.

When Luke was going to school, he won a prize in a raffle - a wind-up racing car.

"It would run around the floor," he recalled, "but one day the key fell down a rat hole in the floor and was never found again. So I had a lovely wind-up car, but it didn't go anywhere."

Maureen remembered the family's weekend routine. Barney worked six days a week. "On Saturday night he'd have his few drinks and on Sunday morning he'd sleep it off. Mam would go to early Mass at the church on Meath Street. If any of the children were awake, she'd tie us on chairs until she got back. It was her way of making sure we were safe and that we didn't disturb Dad before she got back. She'd come in from Mass and get us all ready and dressed up - you had to be spotless - and then you were let out to play. You had to play under the window so she could keep an eye on you. Then she'd start working to get the dinner ready. By then Dad would have gone off to Mass and then in for his Sunday jar. He'd come in and we'd have our dinner. I remember he slipped up one Sunday; he came in drunk but he also came in late."

What followed was part of a trademark of Molly's - that she would hit people with whatever was in her hand. Molly hit him with the plate his dinner was on. She drew blood, and seeing this she ran out in fear, grabbing her daughter Greta, who was then the smallest. She ran downstairs to her neighbour Mrs Madden and stayed there.

"Betty and I were there watching," Maureen said. "wondering what next. Dad sobered up and realised he had been in the wrong. He sent us off to buy cakes in Leary's Bakeries for the tea and he set a lovely table out. Then he sent us down to Mrs Madden to get our Mam to come back up. 'I'm not coming up,' Mam said to us. 'He'll kill me.' We went up and told him this, so he went down himself. We were standing on the landing, listening. He knocked on Mrs Madden's door and she came out. 'Well Barney,' Mrs Madden said, 'what is it'. Barney said 'just tell Molly it's alright and I have her tea ready.' Mam came out then and walked up the stairs past him. We had a lovely tea and scones."

Another time, Barney had promised to bring Molly to a Fair in Harold's Cross. He had gone off while she was making the dinner and was due back by a certain time. But he didn't come back for several hours and when he returned, he was drunk.

"Barney came home and I was arguing with him and I was setting the fire and I turned around and hit him with the poker," Molly said. "I didn't mean to hit him at all. Well didn't I split him and I ran out and I didn't dare come back till he was gone off to hospital. And that night I was sitting at home shaking waiting for him to walk in the door and didn't he walk in with a bunch of flowers for me."

Barney was absolutely extraordinary and exceptional in this. The culture of the time and the way of life in the tenements were completely about the men ruling the women. Physical abuse of women by their husbands was almost routine. Neighbours never intervened, other family members rarely got involved, and if the police were ever called in, the most they would do was to ask the man to quieten down. Alcohol and violence went very much hand in hand in those desperate times of poverty and hardship, yet Barney remained patient and non-violent with his wife and children.

Another exceptional thing about Barney was his attitude to money. Those days were notoriously chauvinistic, and much has been written about men getting paid and then drinking or gambling away most - if not all - their money. Barney would bring his pay home to Molly for her to decide how much could be spared for his pocket money.

"I always remember that Dad gave up his money first," Luke said, "and then he went out with what he had left."

Luke remembered how Barney would always come home and put his pay on the mantelpiece. In 1937, de Valera launched the country's new constitution - which was very much geared towards the primacy of the family and the importance of the woman's place in the home. Barney would certainly have agreed with the values of Dev's constitution. The man, bringing in the money, was seen as the master. But Barney never abused this power and never betrayed his commitment to his wife and children - despite all the hardships and frustrations that he, like his peers, suffered.

A photograph survives from those days. It shows Barney and Molly with four of their five children - only Betty is absent. It is taken against the wall of what is probably the tenement courtyard. Barney, in his early thirties, looks lean as ever but healthy. Molly seems tired, and also appear to be without at least her upper teeth.

"Mammy lost all her teeth early on," Greta recalled. "I don't remember her with teeth when I was growing up. And women those days didn't get false teeth - they couldn't afford them."

The children look clean and well dressed. Maureen holds a toy bucket, Luke a toy spade. Whatever the family event or whoever the visitor was who took the photograph, it gives the impression that the young family were living at least at some level of comfort and well being.

Having lived for years as a couple in this tenement community - and Barney having lived there since his teens - they had many friends. One friend of Barney's was Bill Carroll, who had a shop on the corner of Brabazon Street. Molly said, however, that Barney was very jealous of Bill Carroll. "We would only be sitting together talking," Molly said, "and then Barney would come along and find us and he wouldn't talk to Bill Carroll so Bill would go off."

Molly told the story of how one Sunday she and Barney brought the children to see a film at the Phoenix. Molly had left corned beef in the pot over a very low fire. When they got home, there had been a disaster - the dinner had burned.

"You could look through the hole in the bottom of the pot," Molly said, "and there was nothing to eat for the Sunday dinner."

Maureen remembers a time when Molly's sister Maggie came to them with her son John, who had made his Communion.

"The lad was very shy," Maureen recalled, "and Mammy used to say 'he's stupid, Maggie, and the way you dress him and let his hair go long he's like a runaway monk'. Maggie was very offended and stormed out. Molly called out after her 'I didn't mean it, but you can go way with your runaway monk'. And that became his nickname - the Runaway Monk."

Greta added a twist to the tale.

"Maggie went home and told her husband what Molly had said - and only when he explained what a monk was did she realise it wasn't some kind of monkey. So she went back down to Molly and they had a good laugh about it."

Barney was now getting regular work, as a lorry driver, for a man named Morgan. He often drove down to the Bog of Allen, in Kildare, to collect a load of turf and drive it back to Dublin.

One Sunday, Barney and his brother Peter brought the children Betty, Maureen and Luke out for a drive down to Roundwood in Wicklow in Peter's car. On the way back, they passed through Bray and stopped at a small pub - which happened to be on the incline of a hill. Betty being the eldest, Peter told her "you sit in the front - don't let Maureen or Luke come in."

No sooner were the men gone, than there was a scuffle between the kids. Luke wanted to get into the driving seat. In the scuffle, Luke knocked off the handbrake. The car started to roll down the hill. There were two men walking up the street. One ran around the car, pulled the door open, pushed Luke out of the way, and pulled on the handbrake.

The other man had run into the pub, asking if anyone there had left children in a car outside. Peter and Barney ran out to see the commotion they had caused. By then a policeman had come along and he gave the two men a telling off. The brothers drove straight back home.

Molly gave birth to a son on the 26th of November 1938. He was named Peter, after his father's older brother. There is a three and a quarter year gap between the births of Greta and Peter whereas at that time in her life Molly was having children every one or two years. Some recall Molly saying that in her early years she lost a baby and continued to feel very ill. Then a few days later she was out and started to haemorrhage. She lost a second baby. Medicine of the time was such that they hadn't realised she was carrying twins. Some in the family say that Molly gave birth to the twins and they died before reaching a year old. Betty, however, doesn't remember the twins - and she would have been old enough to do so if they had lived for any length of time in that 1935-8 gap.

Peter's arrival was the start of a ten year period in which Molly, already a mother of five who had suffered the loss of two other children in infancy, would give birth to seven more children. Peter was also the last of the family to be born in Brabazon Street. A whole new world was about to open up for the Duffy family. Tenement life would become a thing of the past.

Barney and Molly with children Maureen, Luke, Freda and baby Greta.

A New Life in Crumlin

At this point in their lives, Barney and Molly had six children and were living in poor conditions in Brabazon Street. At the start of the 1930s two Housing Acts were passed by the government and housing estates were built to the city's north and south in an effort to clear out and pull down the inner city slums. Dublin Corporation offered Barney and Molly a two-bedroomed terraced house in the recently built Crumlin housing estate on the southside.

The estate, on which work had started in 1935, had most of its roads named after Irish diocese; Armagh, Bangor, Clonard, Fogard, Monasterboice, and Leighlin to name but a few. It had been built with a lot of open space and playing fields such as Bangor circle and was a far cry from the cramped inner city life Barney and Molly had been enduring. The Duffys - unlike, for instance, the famous Behans who wrote of Crumlin as a place where 'they eat their young' - welcomed the new opportunity.

Barney and Molly had been given a choice of a few houses on the estate. One, on Sundrive Road, faced a plot where the new Saint Bernadette's Church would be built and Barney said he didn't want to live looking at a church and having the crowds every Sunday. They were offered a house on the short and narrow Kells Avenue, but a friend of Molly's who was living on the estate, Mrs Madden, warned "don't move up there, you're in one and others mouths up there. There's a house idle on Leighlin Road." She gave Molly the number of the house - 147. A family named Fagan had lived in the house and had moved out. The house was on a road that had a large green between it and the houses on the opposite side. Also, there was a large field behind which separated the backs of the Leighlin Road houses from the backs of the houses on Bangor circle. Barney and Molly went into the Dublin Corporation office to ask for it and they were given the house to rent. It would be their home for the rest of their lives.

They moved into the house on September 5th 1939. Maureen remembered the move vividly.

"We loaded our stuff into a pram," Maureen said. "We made about ten journeys, walking back and forth between the Coombe and Crumlin. Mam's sister Maggie lived nearby on Derry Road and came over to help with shifting the things."

With her sister Maggie living nearby, it meant that she and Molly would see each other more often. "If Maggie was arguing with her husband John, she'd come over to Mam," Maureen said.

The move was a transformation in the quality of their lives. They had a livingroom, and a small kitchen-cum-bathroom that people referred to as a scullery. In this room, too, they had their own bath. They had their own toilet too; just outside the backdoor, facing a long garden that was intended to be used for growing vegetables.

"We had facilities in our home that we'd never known before," Luke said. "We had hot running water on demand from the boiler behind the fire - we'd had to boil up water on the fire in the flat. We had electricity - which also meant within a matter of months we got a normal wireless radio plugged into a socket instead of run on the acid batteries bought in the shop on The Coombe. We had a garden at the back AND the front. It was an overnight change to a new way of life."

The previous owners of 147 had painted all the walls yellow and royal blue and the floors were bare stone. The presses had been painted green. Molly set to work redecorating the place and trying to brighten it up. Even though she repainted the deep, cavern-like press in the front bedroom white, Molly always referred to it as 'the green press'.

The two bedrooms were divided into the front room for Molly and the daughters and the backroom for Barney and the sons.

"It was completely different to us, after living in two rooms," Betty said. It also felt like a step up the social ladder. Betty knew a girl named Norton who lived near Brabazon Street, and whose family lived in their own house. Betty always thought they were posh. "And then there we were with our own house and having a garden and everything."

Barney and Molly were moving into 147 Leighlin Road as the Nazis were moving into Germany's neighbouring countries and Britain and France were declaring war on them. It was the start of World War Two - or what in neutral Ireland would be known as 'The Emergency', named after the Emergency Powers Act passed by the Irish government to set up plans for rationing and other restrictions to come. It would mean straitened times for the Irish, but it didn't dampen Barney and Molly's enthusiasm for having babies; they

Barney and Molly

would have five children in the six year course of the war.

"When the war broke out we had nothing to eat," Molly said. "There was a man who came around in a van, and everyone went out with their buckets and he'd shovel a load of fish into the buckets. And that was all we got."

During this time of war, there was rationing of coal and oil in Ireland. Barney had two lorry-driving jobs - for a man named Nugent and another named Morgan - as he struggled to feed and support his family. He was one of the many hired to drive lorries out to the countryside to bring in supplies of turf for Dublin. He did this work with his brother Peter. Because of the fuel shortages of the time, Barney usually drove a lorry that was fuelled by a steam engine and anthracite coal. Luke went with his father a few times on these jobs, and he remembered the terrible stench of the coal.

Given the sprawl of Crumlin - all the houses new and identical - it took a while for Barney to get his bearings. Sometimes, he'd come back in the lorry and drive around trying to remember exactly where he lived.

Molly was pregnant at the time of the move into 147 Leighlin Road. Betty remembered how attentive Barney was to Molly when she was pregnant. When Molly was in labour, Barney would sit with her and hold her hand - until, as was the way those days, he would be told to leave the room by the women who were helping with the delivery. Just a few months in their new Crumlin home, on January 18th 1940, the family had its first new addition when a chubby, healthy baby boy was born. He was named Patrick Ambrose - Paddy - directly after his father's father. Mrs

A New Life in Crumlin

Peg Duffy, the grandfather's widow, was invited to be his godmother. It was the start of a real attachment between the two.

In the same year, Molly's youngest brother, Willie Dowdall, met Maura Harvey. Molly's parents had just moved into 47, Thatch Road in Whitehall, two doors down from the Harveys. Maura's mother was in hospital at the time, and she was looking after the family. Willie's mother saw Maura, and mentioned her to Willie - saying what a remarkable job she was doing in taking care of the children. Mother Dowdall invited Maura into her home, and that's how the romance between Maura and Willie began.

Willie, born in June 1923, was talented, intelligent, but restless. He had spent a brief time in Rockwell College in Tipperary - a short-lived wish to become a priest. He was a late arrival to the family - sixteen years younger than Molly and so born only three years before she married. Willie was bespectacled, thin, creative - and the apple of his mother's eye. Maura was an intelligent and beautiful young woman. Perhaps Mother Dowdall saw in Maura someone who would take care of her son.

"Mrs Dowdall didn't instil a sense of responsibility in her sons," Maura said. "I suspect that all the women in her family were dominant or formidable, but the men were over-indulged."

Mother Dowdall used to give Willie the money to take Maura out for a date. Maura remembers Mother Dowdall as a woman who believed in a lot of Irish superstitions - 'piseogs'.

Maura got to know the Dowdall family. She remembered Willie's sister Maggie as being the most refined. "She was very quiet, and very elegant. She was very small in stature and had very fine features. She had beautiful hands."

Maura remembered the first time she visited Barney and Molly. There was a bus strike on at the time, and she and Willie Dowdall walked from Whitehall on the Northside of Dublin to Crumlin on the Southside.

Peter said that one of his first memories was of his Uncle Willie.

"I'd been taken into hospital to get my tonsils removed," he said, "and the day I was taken home Uncle Willie was there. He lifted me up onto his shoulders so that I could reach the top of the dresser in the front room. He'd hidden a present there for me."

On January 21st 1941, barely more than a year after Paddy's birth, along came another son - this one named William after Molly's brother. Childbirth seems to have become almost routine to Molly.

"I remember Mammy putting up the dinner for everybody," said Betty, "and then saying 'you can call the doctor' and she'd go to bed. The doctor would arrive and the baby would be born in half an hour."

Willie, like Maureen, was born with a 'caul'.

On February 10th 1942 - again little more than a year after Willie's birth - a daughter was born. This child was named Brigid. Barney and Molly probably gave her this name because the feast day of Saint Brigid is February 1st and Brigid - like Patrick - is one of the classic Irish Catholic names. What they may not have known is that they were making an interesting clan connection: Saint Brigid was the daughter of the Leinster chieftain Dubhthach - Duffy. Given that the new baby Brigid was headed for a number of childhood misadventures and mishaps, it's not surprising that she got off to a shaky start. On the morning of her

A New Life in Crumlin

christening, Brigid was crying and Maureen was given the task of soothing her. Maureen held the baby, in the christening gown and blanket, and was rocking her as she paced the floor. Then she noticed - the blanket was empty. Brigid was on the floor.

In her infancy, Brigid had the misfortune of following a family tradition when a rat climbed into her pram and bit her on the nose.

In this prodigious flow of children, it's good to know that Barney and Molly, sleeping in separate rooms, maintained a genuine affection for each other. Breda remembered times when she would see her parents embracing and kissing. They enjoyed being close to each other - they loved each other. That was the engine that kept everything else going and that led them to find a way through every hardship.

Molly's pride and joy was a dresser in the scullery in which she stored all her delph and glasses and other such precious belongings. On the top of the dresser were two large, ornate serving plates. Betty's hair was very long, and one day she was playing near this dresser and her hair caught in a hook of a door. She pulled the whole dresser down on top of herself, smashing most of its contents. "I cried for a month," Molly said.

Luke remembered hearing the crash. The dresser, by design, was built as separate upper and lower parts and he thought it was the weight of the serving plates that had toppled the upper half of the dresser.

Luke was a few months younger than Amby. As Amby grew out of his clothes, his mother used to pass them on to Molly for Luke. Molly was still regularly taking care of Amby so that his mother could work, and

Barney and Molly

a friendship grew between the boys. In the light of this friendship and the tradition of receiving Amby's hand-me-downs, Luke had high hopes when one weekend 'Old Mrs Duffy' arrived up to the house with Amby and a very smart three-wheel bike he had grown out of.

"I was thinking 'great - this'll be left here for me'," Luke recalled. "But by that night when she was going home, she had sold it to our next-door neighbours the Donoghues."

Dowdall brothers and sisters - Luke, Willie, Delia and Maggie - with child Maureen.

By 1943 Ireland had the highest cost of living increase in all of war torn Europe as the isolated country struggled to establish itself. De Valera's Fianna Fail was steering the country towards solid independence, but against great odds. Neither the left nor right wing movements in the country had caught on, and Dev by now had the support of rural, urban and middle class voters. Around this time, too, a loose cannon of the Duffy clan was up to various antics. Eoin O'Duffy, born in Monaghan, was Ireland's fascist leader. Indeed, he once modestly described himself as 'the third most important man in Europe' - after Hitler and Mussolini. He had founded a political movement nicknamed the Blueshirts that was banned. He had gathered a troop of 600 to fight in Spain on the side of fellow-fascist Franco. Fortunately, there is no sign of a family connection to the Duffys of 147 Leighlin Road.

Undaunted by war, poverty and hardship, Molly kept having babies. She gave birth to a big, heavy, healthy son on December 4th 1943. Molly went to the parish priest to ask him a question. She explained to him that she had lost a son Bernard - named after his father - and wanted to know if she could give this new child the same name. The priest said there was no problem with that. There was nothing frail about this Bernard, and he would grow to be the most physically striking of the family - the athlete.

Among the babies and children in 147, Bernard would also earn the unusual nickname 'two teats'. He always had a soother, and sometimes even would crop up with two soothers - one stuck either side of his mouth. A particular trick of his was that if Molly took a soother away from him he would wander off and then return, sporting another soother.

Times were still hard in Ireland: as the Second World War continued, it was causing severe unemployment and scarcity. Even electricity was being rationed.

"There were times you were glad to get a plate of porridge for your dinner," Betty recalled. "People really had nothing. Tea and sugar were rationed, and Mammy used to sell hers on the black market. I remember her weighing ounce bags of tea and sugar to sell. Then she'd get wood and chop it down to sticks and I was sent off door to door to sell it. I remember times out in the rain pushing a box cart selling sticks. Mammy would do anything to keep her home going. She had loans from here and there, but she knew how to stretch every penny."

Through all these times, Barney never gave in to his sometimes bad health. Once, he had been taking a wine-coloured cough lotion to fight off a cold as he could not miss work. When he went to work, however, his boss told him to go home and take a few days off as he was too sick to be working. As Barney was walking up Kildare Road on the way home, he started vomiting. He had taken so much of this cough mixture, however, that his vomit was blood red. Someone witnessed this and immediately phoned an ambulance. He was rushed into James's Street Hospital.

Not far from where the Duffys lived, on Sundrive Road, was some open playing ground and a dump. At least half a dozen wagons a day would arrive there from the electricity generating station at North Wall and dump out waste and ashes.

"There were gangs of kids all round - me included - who would go down and root through the ashes," Luke said. "You'd find cinders and fill up bags with them. Then you could go around door-to-door and sell them for sixpence a bag."

The people used to say "there better not be any clinkers in this lot". Clinkers were pieces that, when they got hot, would fly like bullets out of the fire.

Greta remembered those times too - going down to the dump with Betty to gather cinders, or going out to sell the sticks.

"There's no shame in poverty," Greta said. "Mammy was a great survivor." In later years, the dump was closed and a long and flat-topped hill made from what had been its contents.

Fruit and vegetables were delivered to shops in wooden boxes that were then thrown out, and Molly would send the boys to get these to chop up for sticks.

"There was nothing unusual too," Luke added, "that if you had a nice wooden fence, you might wake up next morning and find your fence was gone. And kids had to be careful that they didn't go back around that road next day selling firewood."

Hard Life and Holes in Pockets

Through the Emergency hardship was accepted and endured by the Irish who - like Barney and Molly - got on with the business of raising families. One thing that certainly would have helped Barney and Molly - now with ten children - was the introduction of Children's Allowance in 1944. It was an effort to help poor people raising large families and was granted for the third and subsequent child under the age of sixteen.

Molly's youngest brother, Willie Dowdall, married Maura Harvey on February 22nd 1944. As bride and groom were under twenty one, they both had to receive written permission from their parents for the marriage. Maura remembers the time as having very strange weather. "We got sunburned out on Bray Head on Saint Patrick's Day, and there was snow in May." Maura and Willie lived with his parents, and Maura soon took on the role of caring for the parents as well as her husband. This went on for some time, but Maura began to feel it wasn't good for the marriage. She felt that herself and Willie should have a home of their own. When she was sitting down for a meal with her parents-in-law, she announced that she and Willie were leaving. Mother Dowdall upended the table in anger.

In 147 Leighlin Road, things were fortunately more enjoyable.

"In those days, before television, families really spent time together," Maura Dowdall said. "In Leighlin Road, people would sit around talking or playing cards or making music. It was full of life."

"Duffys had the name of having the best parties," Peter recalled. "Anyone would want to go to a Duffy's party."

A highlight whenever there was a party was the song 'Sweet Sixteen'. It was Barney and Molly's song.

Maureen fondly recalled one Christmas at Leighlin Road when Mother and Father Dowdall and Willie and Maura Dowdall came up for the evening.

"Father Dowdall was a very quiet and placid man," Maureen said. "You wouldn't get boo out of him. I only remember one time he was boisterous. It was a Christmas night and we were all having a great time with a sing-song and playing cards with Da and having a drink. Father Dowdall was really enjoying himself. But it came time to get the last bus home at eleven. I would always walk down to the bus stop with him." They talked as they walked down to the bus stop on Bangor Road.

"It's terrible cold," Father Dowdall said to Maureen. "It's terrible to have to go out in the cold."

"You don't have to go," Maureen replied.

"Molly wouldn't hear tell of it," he said. "We couldn't go back."

"Say you missed the bus," Maureen suggested. The bus was around at its terminus on Bangor Circle. Standing at the corner of Bangor Road and Bangor Circle, the group could see it there as it pulled away to make its way around to them at the bus stop.

Barney and Molly

When the bus turned the corner off the circle to the road, Father Dowdall stepped out to halt it. The bus duly halted. Then Father Dowdall stepped back.

"Ah feck it," he said.

"Look Da," Willie said, "you're the one who's going to have to throw your hat in."

"I'll throw it in," Father Dowdall said, "and if it doesn't come out - we're in."

The group went back up the road and knocked on the door of 147. Barney opened the door and saw them all before him.

"What's wrong?"

The sitting room door was open and Father Dowdall threw his hat in. Molly came out.

"What's wrong?" she asked.

"The bus went, Molly," he told his daughter. "We couldn't walk home."

"Is there anything we can do," Barney said.

"Molly, you could put us up," Father Dowdall said. "We don't mind sleeping on the floor."

Molly took them in and the festivities continued. Come bedtime, the children were reshuffled and packed in beds to make place in the bedrooms - Willie Dowdall slept downstairs on the sofa. In the morning, Molly made a big fry for everyone. By early afternoon, Molly was starting to prepare the dinner - and Father Dowdall was showing no signs of heading home.

"Look Da," Molly said to him, "it's not going another night - I can't pack the kids like that again."

"Molly was a marvellous manager," Maura Dowdall recalled. During the wartime, Barney worked as a truck driver and the pay was good, but by this time they had ten children ranging in age up to sixteen. "I don't know how she managed. Molly was very helpful to people. I remember her as being a very kind woman."

"Molly had the whole responsibility of how to work out the money," Betty said. "Barney gave her everything he earned, but it was her job after that to stretch the money."

"When we were small, Dad wasn't there all that much," Maureen said. "He'd go out on Monday morning and you wouldn't see him until Friday night. He had his job on the lorries, and the job on the ice cream van working for a man named Capaldi."

"He was always gone before we'd get out of bed in the morning," Luke recalled, "and he was still out working when we were going to bed at night. We really only saw him for a few hours on Sunday morning. So Mam was mother, father and everything else all through the week."

Maura Dowdall remembered Molly as being very strict with her children.

"When the kids were sitting around the table," Maura recalled, "she only had to look at them and they would be on their best behaviour. They were scared of her. Barney was a softie with the kids and she was the disciplinarian."

Barney, indeed, was known for taking a bold child into the next room when Molly said he or she had misbehaved, and then making slapping noises with his hands.

"Daddy was always the soft one," said Greta. "Mam would send him upstairs to us if we were making noise, and he'd come in to the bedroom and tell us Mam had sent him up and ask us to stay quiet or he'd get into trouble."

"Dad had a temper," Peter recalled. "The difference was, if Mam lost her temper - you got it. If Dad lost his temper - he might just walk away."

Sometimes Molly, in all her toothless glory, would rage against a bold child by shouting "I'll ate ya!". Other times, she would make the rather bizarre threat "I'll wool the head off ya!" There were no major casualties in the family, but Molly's rule was firm.

Barney's work, however, was always uncertain. In September 1944, he was let go by the garage PF Nugent, of Parnell Street and Rutland Place. The reference stated; 'Bernard Duffy has been employed by me as Meter lorry driver from 1st July 1942 to 25th August 1944. During this time I found him a good time keeper, honest, capable, and an industrious worker.'

There was no social welfare money in those days. In hard times when people had no work, they were given ration cards for food and other needs. If Barney couldn't find work, he might be sent on 'Relief Work' (something that dated back to the Great Famine and beyond) and you had to do it. Barney worked at times digging ditches or repairing roads. There was no such thing as halting work if it was raining. If you refused the work or stopped working, you lost your benefits.

In those days, people could receive free milk. One of Luke's tasks was to run down every morning before he went to school to the depot - near the police station and Loretto Convent - where it was given out.

"No matter how hard things were," Peter said, "I can never remember a time going without food, or clothes, or a fire. It was only when I married and had children that I realised how difficult that was and how much our parents had achieved. It must have taken one hell of an effort on both their parts. No matter what Dad was earning, it still took a remarkable woman to figure out how to keep us all going."

"We never went hungry," Greta said, "but I think Mammy did."

At the time of Maureen's Confirmation, however, the family was having a particularly difficult time - they didn't have enough money to dress her for the ceremony. Molly was too proud to go ask her mother for help. Maureen told her Mam that it didn't bother her, and just asked her for a note to give to the nuns at the school explaining that she wouldn't be dressed up for her Confirmation. Molly wrote the note.

When the nun read the note, she told Maureen to see her that afternoon over in the convent. Maureen was brought into the parlour and given tea and biscuits and scones - all of which was a treat in itself.

"Your mother wants you to be held back and have your Confirmation next year," the nun said.

"That's right," Maureen replied.

"Do you feel terrible about it?"

"Oh no. If Mam can't afford it then she can't and that's that."

The nun wrote a note and told Maureen to give this to her mother and to meet her at the convent again the following afternoon at the same time. Molly read the note and wrote a reply to it. When Maureen went to school the following afternoon, she gave the nun the note.

"Come back to me on Monday afternoon after school," the nun said when she had read the note. When that day came, the nun brought Maureen into the Arnotts Store in the city centre and dressed her for Confirmation.

"It was nothing fancy," Maureen recalled, "but very nice. I made my Confirmation and I was very proud. I remember that day going up to Mother Dowdall. When we knocked at the door she opened it and looked at us and said 'what do you want?' She didn't even bring us in. I believe Father Dowdall was very cut up about it. But that was her way."

Luke also had an experience of the less-than-generous ways in the Dowdall family. He had made his Communion and Molly had taken him around a few relatives - as was the tradition. She brought him into town where they met her sister Delia.

"Delia rooted in her bag and took out some money," Luke recalled, "then she shuffled the money around in her hands and held out both hands to me and said 'now pick which one the money is in'. I picked the wrong hand - and I got nothing."

Luke remembered an incident from when he was about nine years old. It was not unusual for kids to be going around barefoot - most kids went around so. It was Eastertime, and on Good Friday he went to church to kiss the foot of the Cross.

"A woman in the church saw me and talked to me and she asked me to take her to my home," Luke remembered. "The woman was Betty Fay and she had a clothes shop at the top of Crumlin Road. She asked my mother to take me to her shop, and she clothed me out. She clothed me for a few years after that."

Luke was still going to Francis Street School on the Coombe, and had also become a member of the Boys' Brigade - its meetings held on Church Street at the side of the Four Courts by the River Liffey.

"We had our meetings there in the hall beside the church," he recalled, "and we would go for our Sunday morning parade along there, and we had a marching band."

Caring for the house as well as the children kept Barney and Molly constantly on the go.

"Barney wasn't great around the house," Maura said, "but Molly was great at doing painting and wallpapering. She was very house proud."

Barney did tend the back garden, however. There were blackberry bushes, and he also grew cabbage and lettuce, scallions, onions, cauliflowers, potatoes and radishes through the seasons. Greta was particularly fond of radishes, and would often go out to the garden to pluck them to wash and eat raw.

Barney also didn't often venture out with the children. Nevertheless, Brigid recalls a number of times when he set out with her, Paddy, Willie and Peter to take them to the Zoo.

"Each time, we only got so far," Brigid said, "and then Daddy would stop off for a pint and we'd sit outside with our lemonade and crisps, and when we eventually got going again we'd arrive at Phoenix Park - but we only saw the Zoo from outside because it was closed."

"Don't tell your Mammy," Barney would say to them, and bring them home.

The Sunday morning routine remained the same over the years, with Molly going to early Mass and Barney going later. He would go to the church on High Street for one o'clock Mass, and thereafter go to the pub for a few drinks before going home for dinner. Peter recalled two stories Barney told him about going to Mass there. On one occasion, Barney was standing near the back of the crowded church and someone tapped him on the shoulder and said 'excuse me please'. Barney turned and saw it was an Italian priest he had heard about who was visiting Dublin. Barney stepped aside to let the man pass. Years later, this man became Pope Paul 6th. This seemed like one of Barney's tall tales - but in fact in 1934 Monsignor Montini - future pope - had a brief holiday in Dublin.

The other story is vintage Barney.

"He was standing listening to the Mass," Peter said, "and he looked down on the ground and he saw a threepenny piece - which was a lot of money at the time. He picked it up, and saw there was a collection plate nearby and put the coin on it. After a while, he noticed another threepenny piece. He did the same thing with that. Through the Mass, he found a few more pennies and a sixpence on the ground near him, and he kept putting them on the plate. It wasn't until he came out after Mass that he found he had a hole in his pocket. He had left himself broke."

"Daddy spent more time with friends from the pub than he spent in the pub," Luke said. "After all, the pubs closed at two o'clock on Sunday and there were times he didn't get home until six o'clock. Sometimes I'd even be sent to get him. And what was he doing? Playing cards with his pals. Daddy was very thin and frail - he could never drink very much."

There was a pub in around the Whitefriar Street area, and Barney would have a couple of drinks there, and then play cards outside on the footpath.

"If Dad hadn't shown up for dinner, there were three places I knew to look when I was sent to bring him home," Luke said. "There was a place by Dolphin's Barn, a place off Aungier Street, and a place on Clanbrassil Street. The men would be playing cards -

for pennies or maybe for no money at all - and it could be a job to drag Daddy away from the game. He would always say 'just this last game'."

"Every Sunday, Mrs Duffy and her son Amby would come up, and Uncle Peter and Aunt Mary would come up," Greta recalled. "When you think of how small our house was and with all the children, you'd think it should have been the other way around. But our house was so homely, everyone loved being there. Mrs Duffy used to come with food for herself and Amby."

Georgie Brennan was short, cross-eyed and bow-legged. He was a friend of Barney's as far back as before Barney married, and a favourite card-playing partner. Georgie and his family had also moved to Dolphin's Barn, not far from Crumlin, and he would come to the house every Sunday with cakes from the bakery where he worked. He and Barney would play cards and have a few drinks.

"They would always end up having a sing-song," Greta said. "There were always great sing-songs in the house."

One night, Georgie was to mind his three year old son as his wife was going out. The bottles of porter were out on the table as four men played cards, and as Georgie was having a drink he'd give an occasional drink to the boy who was sitting on his lap. The little boy said he wanted to go to the toilet and Georgie set him down. The boy flopped on the floor. Without realising, Georgie had set the child drunk. Georgie was also too drunk by then to carry the boy home, and Barney had to help him.

On December 9th 1945, a new son came along and he had the unusual distinction of being born with two teeth. This boy was named Kevin - after his father's youngest brother. He was born very weak, and there was a fear that Molly was going to lose yet another child.

"I remember it very clearly," Greta said. "Kevin, like most of the children, was born at home. And I remember it being said that the baby had gone cold, and he was held at the fire." He survived his first hours in this way, but had difficulty breathing.

Molly had heard of something that could help a baby with breathing problems: there were road workers out laying tar on the cracks on the road, and she would take the baby to their work tent so he could breath the tar fumes - it was said to be good for clearing the lungs.

Molly would feed baby Kevin sips of brandy to keep heat in him, and he eventually thrived. The irony of this is that Kevin went on to become the only teetotaller in the family.

In 1946, there was a first in the family - the first extra fulltime wage earner. Maureen was born in 1931, but Molly changed the '1' to a '0' on her birth certificate so that she could get a job in a sewing factory. Breda later also got a job sewing in Cassidy's. She became a cutter - a more qualified job. Breda and the other sisters had a gift for dressmaking.

In the same year, a new milestone was crossed with the first marriage in the family. Betty married Patsy Donoghue on June 9th. Her next oldest sister, Maureen, was bridesmaid. The wedding party was in the house. Luke and the rest of the younger children were deposited with a friend on Kildare Road for the day.

"When I got married, there was no such thing as a wedding cake," Betty recalled. "A friend of Daddy's,

Georgie Brennan, brought a load of cakes. That was his wedding present to us."

A group photo on the wedding day, taken in front of 147, shows many smiling faces. It also speaks volumes about Molly. She is standing at the back row of the group, behind her father. Molly is only thirty nine years old, but looks as old as him. She also looks worn and weary compared to her smiling husband, who stands at the far end of the group beside his brother Peter. Raising eleven children and enduring the hardships of 'the Emergency' had taken a heavy toll on Molly. And yet her child-bearing days were not over and there were many more hardships - and very many more days of endless workload - ahead of her.

For Betty, the wedding marked a break from the family.

"Most of the brothers and sisters were small children when I got married and left home," she said.

Betty's Wedding outside 147

Barney and Molly

It was a break from living under one roof, but simply a new phase in the story of mother and daughter. The bond between Betty and Molly was a particularly strong and complicated one. Betty, named after Molly's mother just as Molly was named after her mother's mother - would go on to have as complicated a relationship with Molly as Molly had with 'Mother Dowdall'. She also would be the only one of Molly's children to have a very big family - she raised nine children, but was pregnant fifteen times - and experience a level of hardship similar to that of her mother's.

Four Generations

By the late 1940s there were four living generations in the family - Mother and Father Dowdall, Molly and Barney, the children of Molly and Barney, and Betty's son Paddy.

Although Betty was living on the North side of town, in Benburb Street, she would visit her mother almost every day. Luke, then in his early teens, had the job of walking her son Paddy home in his pram every evening as Betty had to go on the bus to be home in time to put her husband's dinner on the table when he got home from work.

"The buses wouldn't take prams," Luke said. "There was a place under the stairs of the double decker bus, and if what you had couldn't fit there, then you weren't allowed on. Betty's pram for her son Paddy was too big. So I had this route - I'd go down to cross Dolphins Barn Bridge, then past the Leinster Cinema, and a laneway beside it down to a place we called 'the back of the pipes' and that led out to the back of Guinness's and to Marrowbone Lane to the top of Thomas Street and an old church there. Then I'd go down the hill and across the Liffey to Benburb Street."

As Molly's family grew, her mother had become less happy about being visited by her. In the end she had told Molly "don't come up any more. You have too many kids and they're running around the place." Molly didn't visit her again for years. Despite this, and despite the struggle Barney and Molly were having to raise their family, they gave huge support to Mother and Father Dowdall.

As he had grown old, Luke Dowdall's hair had turned snow white. People nicknamed him 'Father Charles'. He had also mellowed in old age and was a pleasant man.

Despite the struggles of raising her family, Molly would also still keep something aside for her parents. Father Dowdall had been retired from his job at Merchant Warehousing and so the couple became dependent on support from their children.

"We'd go up every Saturday and I'd bring tobacco for my father and tea and bread and butter for my mother," Molly said. "We could have done with it ourselves, but Barney would say 'give it to them - they're old and want it worse than we do', and we'd be starving ourselves." Meanwhile, as it turned out, Mother Dowdall was hoarding any money she could.

"I remember being sent to Mother and Father Dowdall," Luke said. "They were living in a basement flat in the Crescent in Marino. Auntie Delia lived in the flat above them." Molly's sister Delia had married Martin Daly.

Later, Molly's parents moved again - this time further Northside where they lived upstairs in a house that Luke recalled was down a dark alleyway.

"Saturday evenings in particular I remember going to them with food," Luke said.

The chore of going down to Father and Mother Dowdall was shared by the children - none of whom enjoyed the job.

"You had to go down with the pots of cooked food," Peter recalled. "If you were lucky you got a few pence."

Maureen started work as an usherette in the Theatre Royal in 1947. The theatre, built in 1935, had a capacity for an audience of 4,000. It was also a cinema, and it housed the Regal Rooms Restaurant. The theatre had a resident 25-piece orchestra, a marvellous organ that rose from the pit in front of the stage, and a troupe of singer-dancers called the Royalettes. It was a world of glamour for ordinary folk to escape into right in the heart of Dublin. The singer Mary Dowdall, daughter of Father Dowdall's brother Gary, often appeared on stage there and Maureen chatted with her about their respective sides of the family.

Maureen and Friends at 147

Austin Ignatius Gabriel Gibney was a voluntary worker for St John's Ambulance, and was put on duty at the Theatre Royal every Sunday night. There, he met Maureen - and that was the start of their romance.

Austin's father and his uncle, Ignatius - who became a Passionist priest at Mount Argus - were paternal twins. Austin was from his father's first marriage. Austin's mother died when he was a child and his father remarried. This wife did not accept the duties of raising Austin, and he was partially raised in another family. As Austin grew up, there was decreasing contact between him and his father's new family. He was very struck, therefore, by the close-knit nature of the Duffy family. In meeting Maureen, he had also been embraced into a big and busy family life and he enjoyed this very much.

Maureen and Austin were a handsome and lively pair. Maureen was beautiful - she had even been in the Dawn Maid beauty contest - and Austin, with his Clark Gable moustache and great capacity for tall tales, was a charmer.

"Austin was very dapper and a real lady's man," Maura recalled. "He was very handsome and had a charm about him." The funny thing is, Austin had once flirted with Maura, not knowing she was dating his girlfriend's uncle. "When he met me in Leighlin Road, he nearly died."

On August 30th 1947, Molly gave birth to another daughter. This child was born at home in the middle of the night. Given that by then the house was swarming with kids, it's not entirely surprising that next morning no one was paying a great deal of attention to the new arrival as they were getting ready for school or work. Maureen was about to sit in a chair when Barney shouted 'the baby!' Maureen had almost sat on her new sister.

Now Molly and Betty, mother and daughter, would walk down the road each pushing prams.

Four Generations

The wife of Molly's Uncle Barkel, Ethel, had died and Barkel made a proposal to Molly and Barney regarding their new daughter. If they would name the child Ethel, Barkel would sponsor her - providing for her clothing and other needs. Barney was against the idea - he didn't like the name 'Ethel'. Molly, however, looked at it more practically. And so the name was chosen.

Ethel was born with a full head of hair - so much so that when she was brought to be baptised the priest complained to Molly and Barney for taking so long to bring a child for christening. She was duly baptised with the chosen name: a name, however, that would eventually cause problems for Ethel.

"Everyone else in the family had normal Irish names," Ethel said, "and at the end of all this comes an 'Ethel'. To make things worse, Barkel didn't stick to his side of the deal." After a couple of years, he had forgotten his promise. But Ethel still carried the name.

"That name!" Barney would later say, throwing up his hands. "A Protestant name!"

Years later in school, Ethel was often asked what saint she was named after.

"I would be left standing against the wall, dumb," Ethel said, "with no saint I was named after that I could talk about."

Life and child-rearing in 147 went on. The gang of young children meant a strict morning regime. Each had to get themselves clean and combed and well wrapped against the weather, then they would line up at the door. Molly would then inspect the line-up and give each in turn a spoonful of either emulsion or castor oil.

Sometimes, to help the medicine go down, she'd also give them a spoonful of sugar.

"Sometimes she'd hold your cheek in her finger and thumb and really squeeze," Peter remembered, "as if she'd take a lump out of you."

Through all this, Molly also suffered ill health. Greta remembered a time when Molly had an ulcer on her leg and a nurse - Nurse Rowe - would have to come to treat it. "They made a kind of makeshift stretcher for Mammy in the front room," Greta recalled, "and the treatment was that the nurse would scrape away the ulcers."

As the family was growing up, Molly delegated whatever work she could. Willie recalled a time when one of the more bizarre family traditions resurfaced. The older brothers and sisters had been given the task of polishing the floor and furniture as Barney and Molly went out. They tied the younger ones to chairs until the parents came home so that the place would look perfectly clean.

Brigid, at the age of five, suffered an accident that would have a serious effect on her.

"Breda had been sent on a message to a friend of Mammy's, a Mrs Lennon, who lived on Kildare Road," she recalled, "and she had me by the hand walking along with her. There was a wall along the front of the gardens there, and I was a bit smaller than the wall. An Alsatian dog jumped over the wall - and over my head - and with the fright I got, my left eye turned in completely and my right eye slightly." From then on, Brigid was what people called 'gunner-eyed'. This was exactly what Molly had tried to become long before as a child. Seeing it now in her daughter, Molly was not so taken with the idea of having such a condition.

Four Generations

Some more of the family were reaching the age where they had completed a minimal education and could start work to help finances in the home. Luke finished school at the age of thirteen. He had not gone to the local Christian Brother school but instead to Larkfield School where he had been taught by lay teachers, and as a result had also missed out on half a year's education in 1946 because of a strike by national teachers. Luke's first job was in a clothing factory on Abbey Street - earning five shillings a week. He worked as a messenger boy also for McKearns Motors on Tara Street, and later got a job at Caffola's ice cream factory in Santry.

As with the others, Greta finished school when she was thirteen. She then got her first job, sewing, for Burton's. Her birth certificate was also altered so that she would officially be old enough to work. She later worked in a sewing factory called the Bespoke, on Cork Street. This meant she was near where Molly's parents lived, and Greta would drop in and do some cleaning around for them.

"Mother Dowdall was a great one for finding out information," Greta said, remembering one incident.

"What's Molly saying about me," Mother Dowdall asked her.

"She's saying nothing," Greta replied.

"Come on girl," Mother Dowdall coaxed her.

Finally Greta said "she just says you're an auld ram, but she doesn't say anything else."

Mother Dowdall threw Greta out.

"When I went home and told Mammy," Greta recalled, "she nearly killed me. But you see - I didn't know what a ram was."

Brigid, like all the Duffy girls, was going to the Holy Faith Convent on the Coombe. This was just around the corner from Clanbrassil Street where Mother and Father Dowdall lived.

"At lunch time we had to stay in the school grounds," she said, "and I often thought how great it would be to have a nice Granny and Granda so I could go around to them and sit with them at lunch."

"Mother and Father Dowdall were like Mammy and Daddy," Betty said. "He was the gentle one, and she was the hard one."

"Mother Dowdall was contrary," Greta said, "whereas Father Dowdall was very soft and kind."

Molly's sister who lived nearby, Maggie, died in 1948, leaving behind her husband, named Burke, and three children.

Maureen and Austin told the story that at the funeral Father Dowdall, as he stood by his daughter's grave, was stung by a wasp. He ignored the sting, but it became infected and began swelling more and more. By the time he went to a doctor, gangrene had already set in and the leg needed to be amputated. They said too that the amputation had to be carried out, in the Meath Hospital, with Father Dowdall in his full senses because he had a weak heart and they could not risk giving him a general anaesthetic. Mother Dowdall sat outside on the steps of the hospital during the operation, waiting until he was brought back to the ward.

This is the kind of yarn that made Maureen and Austin such an entertaining couple. A more plausible story - though far less colourful - is that the injury happened over a period of time. Father Dowdall had to wear steel-cap boots in work and he got a cut in his toe. The polish on the boot made its way into the cut, and the cut became infected. Treatment for this started too late, and the infection started to spread up his leg. There were a series of operations - his foot was removed, then his leg below the knee - until finally his entire leg was removed.

"He was also a smoker and had heart problems," Greta pointed out. "Maybe what happened was due to blood circulation problems." This may very well be true, for Brigid recalls that by the end of the man's life the infection was in his other leg.

Molly's parents had been living in a flat over the Banba book shop on Clanbrassil Street. When Father Dowdall became wheelchair bound, his wife would wheel him around. "He wouldn't let me wheel him," Molly said. "Nobody was allowed to wheel him but my mother."

Mother and Father Dowdall

When Father Dowdall lost his leg, it became difficult for the old man to get out and about and he spent most of his time confined to the flat looking out the window. Not that Father Dowdall took his problem too much to heart. One time, Luke was visiting his grandparents delivering food and supplies.

"I was looking out and I saw a man down there with no legs," Father Dowdall said to Luke. "He was arrested by the police."

"What did they arrest him for?" Luke asked.

"Well - he was arsing around."

Finally, the old couple moved home yet again. They moved to a cottage at 7, Pembroke Street in Irishtown, becoming neighbours of Barney's brother Peter and wife Mary who lived in number 5. Mary had heard about the flat becoming vacant and had gone to the landlord to get the flat for the old couple. Barney and Molly's helping Mother and Father Dowdall continued - now with a new venue for the children making the deliveries.

On Barney's side of the family, another relative remained in the fold. Barney's father's widow, Mrs Peg Duffy, was a frequent visitor with her son Amby. Her godchild, Barney and Molly's son Paddy, had remained a particular favourite of 'Old Mrs Duffy'. She was concerned, however, about his place in the home because she felt he was often bullied by his brothers. "Paddy was a very kind person," she recalled. Paddy would sometimes visit her and she would make him a meal.

She recalled also that Peter was having some problems at home and that at one stage he ran away. A few days later, a policeman found him sleeping on a bench by Sandymount Strand. The Garda took him back to the Irishtown barracks and gave him a meal and asked him to promise not to run away again. Peg Duffy wound up finding out about this because, coincidentally, the Garda involved, a man named Fox, was an acquaintance of hers and mentioned the case to her in passing.

The friendship between Amby and Luke had also continued. Luke remembered times when he and Amby would race each other along Landsdowne Road wanting to be like the new Olympic gold medal Czekoslovakian runner, Emil Zátopek.

Barney and Molly's son Willie was always in some way attached to trouble.

One time, Molly was at the door chatting with neighbour Mrs Donoghue when she saw the peculiar sight of a man cycling along with a boy covered in mud and weeds on the crossbar of the bike. Molly thought the boy looked somehow familiar.

"God help that young fella when his mother sees him," she said to Mrs Donoghue. Then the cyclist swerved back. Willie had just realised they had passed his house. Willie had been playing down by the canal and had fallen in. The man had fished him out and was bringing him home. Being born with a 'caul' may have saved Willie from drowning. It didn't save him from Molly's wrath.

"Mam then gave me a belt on the ear for falling into the water," Willie recalled. "She said 'get in there ya stupid git ya'."

Brigid, meanwhile, had another accident. One evening, when she was six years old, she was taking Kevin out to the toilet. She had opened the back door leading to the toilet, and to reach up to turn on the light in the toilet she had to stretch up, while at the same time her hand was in the jam of the back door. Just then, Breda opened the front door as she arrived home from work. It was a very windy night, and the back door slammed shut on the top of the little finger of Brigid's right hand.

"There was blood everywhere," Brigid recalled. Breda rushed down to the hospital with Brigid and Molly followed - she had discovered a piece of Brigid's finger and had brought it in a match box. It was too late for the hospital to be able to do anything with it.

Maura and Willie Dowdall became good friends with Maureen and Austin. Maura also made Brigid's Holy Communion dress - beautifully done with white lace and a satin belt. On the day of Brigid's Communion, Breda brought her to the church and afterwards to the school where the children were served cake and lemonade. Brigid spilled raspberry lemonade down the front of her dress.

"Breda nearly died with fright," Brigid recalled, "trying to find some way to wash it off before Mam saw it."

Through working in the Royal - and being such an outgoing and cheery young woman - Maureen made many friends. She regularly brought friends to the house from the Royal, and there were many parties.

"Maureen was very popular," Greta recalled. She and Austin were very much the golden couple, and there are photographs of them from around this time that show Austin gadding about on a croquet lawn and the couple in the company of very glamorous acquaintances.

Barney and Molly regularly had get-togethers - hoolies - that were fondly remembered. Molly, in her forties, would still get up and dance a hornpipe.

"And Barney could still flirt," Maura recalled with a laugh. "Barney was something else - a real charmer. I wasn't the only woman who fell for Barney - he was very much a lady's man."

Barney worked ceaselessly, but he was not happy with his job driving the ice cream van. He worked with a woman named Greene who lived on Clonard Road, and the job involved driving around the Crumlin housing estate. Barney was always concerned about the children who would rush to the van, and much preferred the lorry driving work that would take him on long hauls to the countryside. One day, Barney's worst fears were realised. A boy suddenly ran out of nowhere onto the road and the van struck him. There was nothing Barney could have done about it - but he was deeply upset to have hurt a child. Despite the difficulties of finding work, Barney quit the ice cream van job.

In 1949 Barney finally managed to find steady employment, working in Santry for the car assembly company Buckley's. His brother Paddy was working there and told him about a vacancy. Assembly plants - for cars and other things - were a common source of employment in Ireland. This was due in part to a British policy of blocking industrial development in Ireland. Also, wages in Ireland were far lower than in England - it was England's Third World next-door-neighbour. Barney was a devout trade unionist - though he drew the line at being in any way Leftist. He also knew only too well the realities of the work situation.

Molly's childbearing days seemed to be over. A mystery that remained, however, was how two people who slept in separate bedrooms in a house swarming with children of all ages were managing to procreate. The secret may lie in film.

"Every Saturday afternoon," Brigid said, "we were all sent off to the Bower picture house (later the Apollo Cinema, on Sundrive Road). It was fourpence in for the wooderners - the wooden seats - and you got tuppence to spend. You were always sent early so you'd be top of the queue." This wasn't a time when Barney was down the pub and Molly polishing the floor. This was a time when the house was cleared out so Barney and Molly could be alone.

"You were sent and you went," Ethel said. "It was the only time they had on their own." It was a tradition that went on for years, with always the older ones given responsibility to take care of the younger ones.

Luke remembered also a shop beside the Bower, 'Ma Henry's', where he would buy cigarettes. He was too young to buy cigarettes, and the old woman who owned the shop had an unusual marketing trick.

"You had to buy hair oil as well as cigarettes," Luke explained. "The hair oil came in small glasses - like phials. I would buy Woodbines - she had them in packets of two or four cigarettes - and this hair oil too. I wound up with tons of the stuff at home."

The cinema also had an alternative system of payment that was typical of the hard times; entry could be bought for the price of so many empty bottles or jam jars. There were refund credits on such items that were accepted in place of the few pence that entry cost.

Barney's brother Peter and wife Mary had a car and sometimes they would pick up Barney and Molly to drive them out to Portrane beach. Maureen recalled one time when she was invited along. Mary was a very straight-laced person and Peter a teetotaller and their choice of where to go for some fresh air was well planned. "Don't worry about Barney," Mary said to Molly, "there's not a pub for miles anywhere around here."

After a half hour or so, Barney said to Maureen, "come on and we'll go for a walk," and off they set.

They walked along the beach maybe a mile and then Dad looked back.

"They can't see us," he said. He cut across over the dunes and Maureen, mystified, followed. They came to a small narrow turning - there was nothing in sight anywhere. Then into view came a little cottage. Barney went up to it and just lifted the latch on the front door. He pushed the door open.

"Daddy," Maureen said to him, "you can't just go in to someone's home like that."

She followed him in, and started to hear voices. They had gone in the back entrance of a pub.

"To the day she died," Maureen recalled with a laugh, "Mary never knew we'd been in a pub that day."

The decade ended with the completion of a long process for Ireland as it had gone from its initial independence through being a 'free state' and 'Eire'. On April 17th, a few days after Molly's 42nd birthday, a 21-gun salute on O'Connell Bridge marked the country's official departure from the British Commonwealth and its official establishment as the Republic of Ireland. All this had been largely driven by Barney's hero, de Valera - even though this event happened when Dev's Fianna Fail party were not in power.

The Fifties Begin

In the early years of their marriage, Barney and Molly had lost two of their children to the hardships of the Dublin of the time. As the new decade began, the couple were suddenly in danger of losing a third: this time, to the State. Brigid had suffered two accidents - the fright affecting her eyesight and the door slam taking off part of a finger. These had required medical care and, as a consequence, time missed from school. But there was someone monitoring this: someone who took no time to investigate the reason behind Brigid's absenteeism. Barney and Molly were served with a notice stating their daughter Brigid would be taken from them and put into a children's home.

"I was out of school once a month or so going to the Eye and Ear Hospital," Brigid said, "and then the accident with Kevin meant even more time out of school and I was a long time attending hospital with that - the dressing being changed to see how it would heal up. There was a lot of bleeding, and I had to keep my right hand - my writing hand - held up in a sling. To make things even worse, I also had an ear infection that left me deaf for a while in one ear. I had to go to the Richmond Hospital twice a day to get injections against the infection. An abscess grew in my ear, and this had

The Fifties Begin

to be drained twice a day also - hoping that I wouldn't permanently lose my hearing in that ear."

All of this meant Brigid was missing a lot of school.

In those days there were school inspectors who would go from school to school looking up the roll books and checking on attendance and grades. In Crumlin, there was an inspector who had noticed Brigid's absenteeism. He finally brought a summons to Barney and Molly over their daughter's poor attendance rate in school. They were brought to court, with their right to keep Brigid at home at stake. The summons stated that Barney and Molly were to attend the court with Brigid and to come with her 'prepared' - with a bag of clothes and belongings. She could be taken from them that very day.

"I can remember sitting outside in a big corridor in the court," Brigid said. "I remember how huge everything seemed to me - the big brown shiny seats. I remember Mam and Dad being called in."

Barney and Molly went armed with letters from the various hospitals and doctors explaining Brigid's various health misfortunes and showing that Brigid had missed school for good reasons.

When Brigid regained her full health, she went on to win prizes for her attendance and grades in school. But it was a terrifying time for her and her parents.

Every now and then, baffling larger-than-life tales crop up in the family. One of these is Bernard's story about 'the American Uncle'. Barney had told the children that an uncle of his from America was visiting Ireland and would visit Leighlin Road. Bernard remembers being told that this man would arrive in a chauffeur-driven limousine. All the children were cleaned up and put in their best clothes. Bernard and Kevin sat together on the railings waiting for the limousine to arrive. A small black Ford Prefect came along.

"The funny thing is, he did have a chauffeur," Bernard said. "This small, grey, stooped, wizened man got out - he looked two hundred years old. He spoke like John Wayne. It was just a short visit, and then he left. And that was it. I remember Kevin and I looking at each other, completely baffled."

There were other far flung relatives who maintained contact. A couple of times a year, Molly's Uncle Jim in Australia would send home money for the children. He had never married and had no children.

"We'd each get a half a crown," Brigid said, "which was a huge amount of money for us in those days."

Paddy's First Communion

The Fifties Begin

In July 1951, Barney and Molly celebrated their twenty fifth wedding anniversary. Their marriage was the engine that drove all the life around them, and they were a happy couple. They had weathered tragedy, hardship, loss and poverty. But they were together and they were raising a healthy, close-knit family. The decade ahead would see many of their children leave the nest of 147.

The couple had a big party at home to celebrate their wedding anniversary, and the house was full with family and friends. Greta was dressed up for the party, and was also wearing lipstick and make-up. Molly's sister Delia started criticising Greta, telling her to get rid of the make-up, and Greta became more and more annoyed. Finally, Greta had an untypical outburst and said to her Aunt Delia "you go off out of that - sure your face and my arse matches."

An argument flared up, but Greta might have thought more about who exactly was insulted: Delia, a lifelong heavy smoker, had a thin, pale, grey, deeply lined and wrinkled face.

Bernard and Kevin were very close and always played together. Bernard remembered a time when he accidentally broke Kevin's leg.

"I was walking on the railings that were along the back of the houses around the field, and for some reason Kevin was lying on the ground," Bernard said. "I lost my balance and fell - and landed on his leg. He was screaming in agony and I was looking at him thinking 'I'm going to get in trouble for hurting him'. Kevin couldn't get up. I made him crawl all the way across the field to our house. I was seriously killed by Mam."

On a brighter side, the brothers also had their party piece - performing 'The Laughing Policeman'. Another song in the same vein, with the opening lines 'I went to your wedding, although I was dreading...' was a regular part of their repetoire.

"Bernard had the heartiest laugh," Ethel recalled. "The tears would be rolling down their faces."

The boys went to Saint Coilm's Christian Brother School on Armagh Road. Willie remembered it as a place where fights could easily start between the kids - but then Willie was quick to take up any challenge. "All the kids were rough and tough," he said. "You had to be, just to get by."

"Bernard minded me a lot," Kevin said. "Being that bit older, no one dared to do anything with me because he'd beat the shit out of them. It was great because we were the Duffy clan - Paddy, Willie and Bernard were there - and nobody would dare touch us."

Paddy, typically, was a good boy in school. One annual report card showed that he had almost perfect attendance; he had been absent just one half day in the entire year. A Christian Brother had written in beside the half day 'what a pity'.

On a small green on the way up to the school was a shop kiosk owned by a blind man. He had a very elegant and educated voice. He did not wear something like the dark glasses often worn by the blind, so one could see his sightless eyes. He sold sweets, cigarettes, ice cream, and some groceries. He knew exactly where everything was in the kiosk, and knew the feel of every coin. There was a small window hatch, and he stood behind that from morning until late in the evening.

Beyond that, on the crossroads before the school, women would be out with prams from which they sold bags of broken sweets and rock to the children on their way to and from school.

"The school was wild," Bernard said. "One incident I always recall was that a boy in our class made the mistake of saying he was an atheist and that his Dad was an atheist. The Christian Brother we had at the time was a replacement for our usual Brother. He took the boy to the top of the class, stood him on a chair, and whipped his legs with a leather strap - blood was drawn. The strange thing is that we kids were cheering. Next day, a knock came to the classroom door. The Brother went out, and we heard raised voices in the corridor. Next we heard crash-bang-wallop. The boy's Dad had come up and laid this Brother cold."

Bernard himself had no bad memories of the school.

By then, Crumlin was bursting at the seams with children, teenagers, and young people. The field on Leighlin Road could at times be completely full with kids and groups. Poverty was extreme, and Crumlin was a rough place.

"You often couldn't play football out on the field," Willie recalled, "because there were too many people out there. It seemed like every house had at least six or seven kids."

"I think everyone who came to our house was overawed by the size of the family," Bernard said. "There was also so much going on. I remember the sisters sitting every evening cutting out patterns and sewing clothes - you'd see a pattern on the floor one day, and a few days later it would be a new dress. The place was always busy."

By then, too, the sisters were making dresses for Molly, who had always put clothes for herself far down the list of priorities in caring for the family.

"I have lovely memories of the Summer holidays, with all the girls sitting in sewing circles," Brigid said. "Breda used to bring home off-cuts of material from where she worked and give them to me and my friends. We'd sit out on the field and make rag dolls. Mammy would give us wool to make their hair, and we'd draw their faces. Then we'd make clothes for them through the Summer."

Some people were struggling to survive. Brigid recalled that there was a spot at the front of the front garden - near the gate - where Molly would put the ashes from the fire.

"I saw a woman from down the road coming into our garden and raking over the ashes looking for cinders for her fire," Brigid said. "She'd put them into a bag for her fire, where we were getting that bit more comfortable and didn't have to gather every cinder."

"Everyone was the same," Molly said. "We were all struggling. The only ones who had money were the Conways, because Mrs Conway was a moneylender." Borrowing money was an art Molly needed to master. The pawnshop had long been a standard part of weekly life - clothes, sheets, cutlery were all in a regular traffic in and out of the pawnshop on the corner of South Circular Road and New Street.

"Things went in on Monday and came out on Friday," Willie said. "The challenge for Mam was always to get through to Friday." Willie also recalled having to collect things from Betty to pawn them for her.

Barney knew that his good suit was pawned on Monday and taken out on Friday, but he never talked openly about it. If he needed it for some reason, he would simply say 'there's a union meeting on Thursday night,' and that would be Molly's notice that the suit had to be out of the pawn for him.

"If you tore your trousers and the arse was out of it," Kevin said, "then you got a patch - not new trousers. And I remember going to school with cardboard in my shoes. Everything from schoolbags to clothes were all passed down. It was even a way of measuring how grown up you were getting - 'I'm big enough to fit Peter's trousers'."

Even a prayer book had gone from Peter to Paddy to Kevin - each brother in turn scratching out the previous owner's name and address and writing in their own name and - of course - the same address.

"I was in short trousers until I was about twelve," Bernard said. "You wound up being in clothes until you'd really grown out of them."

There had always been plenty of music, dancing and celebration in Molly and Barney's life. For Molly a favourite visitor was her youngest brother, Willie. He was a talented musician. Molly and Barney had a piano, and Willie Dowdall would play it. Peter taught himself how to play piano, and there were times when the two would sit together and play.

"My brother Willie was a great pianist," Molly said. "He could make the thing talk. I remember that when he'd come to visit after being a long time away, he'd open the door and throw his hat into the living room first as if to say if his hat was welcome he was welcome."

Willie Dowdall and his wife Maura, however, had suffered tragedy and misfortune. Willie, a highly gifted violinist as well as a pianist, had auditioned for a place as violinist in the Radio Eireann Light Orchestra, but wasn't chosen. Through the help of a friend of Maura's, he got a job as manager of the spare parts department in McKearn's Motors in Santry. It was solid work for a family man, but he could find no outlet for his musical talents.

Maura and Willie Dowdall

In August 1950, Maura gave birth to a son. He was named Luke after Willie's father. Three and a half months later, the baby died. August of the following year, Maura gave birth to another boy. He was named William, after his father. The boy was healthy and it seemed that with a steady job and the beginning of family life things would go well for the couple. Within a year, however, strains on the marriage became too much for the couple and they separated.

Later, Willie Dowdall found a flat in the house where his parents were living in Pembroke Street.

The Fifties Begin

Entering the hall door of the house, his flat was the door to the left and theirs was the door to the right. Luke would sometimes visit his Uncle Willie and remembers Willie's part in the family's ongoing interaction with rats.

"There were lots of rats around the place," Luke recalled, "and Uncle Willie had a pellet gun. One of his favourite hobbies was to hunt them with his pellet gun - and he got a few."

As time went on, Brigid's problem with her eyes became a source of disagreement between Molly and Barney. Molly had gone to the hospital many times with Brigid, and had been told that an operation could be performed. But its success could not be assured - indeed, it could drastically worsen the situation.

"Daddy didn't want me to have the operation," Brigid recalled, "because there was a risk I could be left blind. Dad's attitude was that the sight I had was better than no sight. Mam's argument was that I was a young girl and what chance would I have in life if I didn't have my eyes straightened."

"With so much poverty and so many children, I think it was remarkable that Mammy had something done about Brigid's eye," Greta said.

The operation finally happened.

"I remember Mammy bringing me into the hospital, and that she came to see me every day," Brigid said. "I remember very clearly being in the hospital - and that there were a few country kids in the ward who wouldn't have any visitors at all. I remember being a bit more adventurous and going around from ward to ward and the nurses bringing me by the hand. Daddy hadn't been in to see me, and every day when Mammy came in I asked after Daddy - I knew there was friction between them over the operation. I was even afraid to sleep during the day, in case my Da would come in. When I went asleep my eyes would stick - and I was afraid my Daddy would come in and think I was blind and would go home giving out to Mammy. Daddy never came in to visit me."

After the surgery, Brigid was seeing double. It was still so when she was allowed home, and Barney was getting very agitated and upset about it.

"There was a man who lived in a cul-de-sac across from us, a Mister Cullen, and all the kids loved him," Brigid said. "I was home from hospital a few days and I was standing at the window in the front room looking out and I remember shouting out 'Mammy Mammy! There's two Mister Cullens!'"

It took weeks before finally Brigid stopped seeing double. But then came a new problem.

"Sometimes, Brigid would wake up with a pain in her eye," Greta recalled, "and if that happened then everyone would scatter because that meant Brigid was going to be sick."

"Me eye me eye me eye," Brigid would shout, in the middle of the night.

"I remember a time when Breda and Maureen were at the top of the bed and I was sleeping at the bottom," Brigid said, "and Greta was sleeping in the bed with Mammy. Ethel was in a little fold-up bed in the middle. I woke up and sat up. 'What's wrong?' someone said. 'I've a pain in me eye,' I said. And there was a scatter in the room before I threw up."

Greta went to the New Year's celebration at the Olympic Ballroom at the end of 1951, and there met

The Fifties Begin

Tom Carroll - a young man who lived not very far away from her on Crumlin Road. He was training as an electrician in the Guinness brewery, where his father also worked. Tom was a fan of jazz and played bass as a hobby. It was another Duffy marriage in the making, but it had a long way to go yet.

The Change of Life is Kicking

Luke was working often with Betty's husband Patsy on cars in the evenings and at weekends. But this led to a problem.

"He did car repairs, and I used to strip down the engines," Luke said. "My job was to clean everything out with paraffin oil and he would repair whatever needed repairing. It wound up, though, that we'd be drinking together nearly every weekend. As time went by, it became too serious and I decided to take the pioneer pin and stopped drinking."

For years afterwards, Luke didn't drink alcohol. The experience gained through Patsy, however, helped Luke qualify for work in the motor trade.

In 1952, Luke started work with his father in Buckley's car assembly plant in Santry. Barney's position on the assembly line was hanging doors. These were big, heavy doors and Luke used to argue with Barney saying that, as he was approaching fifty, he should try to find lighter work. Barney said he couldn't find other work and was glad to have a steady job.

"We had a good relationship," Luke said. "We used to play cards, we used to cadge cigarettes off each other. Solo was a popular card game played during lunch hour, and I finally got the go-ahead to join the game."

The Change of Life is Kicking

Barney was always an excellent card player, and could also be critical if he saw people making what he knew was a bad move. In the game, each person called out the number of 'tricks' they had in their hand. This might be five or six. One time, Luke called thirteen - the maximum possible. Although there were only pennies riding on these bets, to call thirteen could leave Luke more than broke.

Barney looked at Luke.

"Are you sure?" he said to his son.

"Definitely," Luke replied. "Thirteen with the trump." This meant he could not be beaten. Luke put one of his cards away and took the trump card. He then lay down his cards; he had the full set of thirteen diamonds.

A bond between Barney and Luke grew that was even more than father and son - they became friends. This then, naturally, led to some ribbing between the two. At that time, Luke cycled to and from work, whereas Barney got a lift into town from a friend and then got the bus home. A debate grew between father and son as to which way home could be the quickest, and they decided one day to put it to the test - with Barney betting two cigarettes that he would be home the quickest.

Luke got on his bike and pedalled as fast as he could, speeding from the Northside, down through town, and south to Crumlin.

"I got home, and I was putting the bicycle in the garden - under the window where I always put it - and the next thing, a car pulled up and Dad stepped out. The man had given him a lift all the way home," Luke recalled. "He'd tried to pull a fast one on me."

Barney lost his two cigarettes.

When he was twelve, Paddy caught primary tuberculosis and was taken into hospital. Paddy was a helper on the Premier Dairy milk lorries, and at that time the helpers weren't allowed to sit in the cabs with the drivers: they had to stand up on the back of the lorry. On a particularly bad morning, he had been soaked through and as a result caught a bad cold. This turned into pneumonia that then turned into tuberculosis. He was in hospital for several months. The neighbour Mrs Mardi was a cleaner working in the hospital and kept a special eye out for Paddy to see he was well cared for.

When Paddy was struck by this life-threatening illness, Molly was told to bring all her children, from Peter down, into a clinic in Lord Edward Street for vaccination. Each child was given a special plaster placed on their chests and they were to come back a week later for a reaction to be tested. In the course of that week, Brigid noticed she had a little rash under her plaster whereas the others had no reaction. Her brothers and sister were jeering Brigid, saying she would have to get an injection. When they went back to the clinic, it was Brigid who was spared the injection. The rash indicated that she was not in danger of her contracting tuberculosis.

After his months in hospital, Paddy was sent to a nursing home called Linden for several months. Greta recalled that while he was there, as part of therapy for the patients, he made chalk ornaments. He gave one of the ornaments to the mother of Greta's new boyfriend Tom Carroll.

The Change of Life is Kicking

"I remember going up to the nursing home," Brigid said, "and it was beautiful. There were peacocks running around the grounds."

When Paddy came home, Barney and Molly had been told that he could not sleep in a crowded room, so they got a sofa bed for him downstairs in the sitting room on his own. Once he recovered, Paddy was back being his 'softie' self again. He did voluntary work for St Vincent de Paul, and would visit the elderly. It used to annoy Barney that Paddy was so soft.

"You're just a big eejit," he would say to Paddy - although Barney was probably the biggest 'softie' of them all. Barney often got annoyed with Paddy - telling him to take his hands out his pockets, and stand straight, and stop shuffling his feet.

"Paddy was a softie," Greta said. "If you were rushing out to go on a date, Paddy would be the one who'd polish your shoes for you or go and get something for you. I never remember seeing him in bad humour. Never."

Greta also recalled that Paddy suffered from smelly feet. He would willingly go out to the back yard to take his socks off and wait there for a few minutes for the smell to fade before he'd come back in.

Paddy was back at school and work, rejoining the Duffy hectic family life. Mrs Mardi, who lived on Leighlin Road, took a shine to Paddy through the time he had been in hospital and would often take him in to feed him.

Paddy's Uncle Peter and Aunt Mary gave him a gift after he recovered; a Kerry Blue terrier. This little black dog was the same kind that Barney and Peter's father had bred. The dog was named Tiny, and he became more than part of the family. He became devoted to

Barney, who in turn said that Tiny was not to be allowed out wandering around like other dogs in the area.

"Tiny was always a house dog and was always playing with us," Brigid said. "When he got tired of playing with us, his favourite place was to go out to the foot of the stairs in the hall and have a rest there on a little mat. If anyone put their foot inside the gate, the dog would bark."

Molly was approaching her 45th birthday in 1952. She had, by then, given birth to fourteen children as well as having some failed pregnancies - including twins. In all, it is believed she had been pregnant an astounding nineteen times. Her youngest child, Ethel, was almost five. Ethel was the last in a series of children Molly had given birth to at a rate of almost one a year since the move to Crumlin and was the little princess in a family that was starting to get past the worst of its hardships with some young breadwinners now helping to share the financial burden. Molly was also putting on weight and had been diagnosed with diabetes. It was the beginning of old age and the end of childbearing.

When she realised she hadn't had a period for a couple of months, however, Molly went to the Coombe Hospital with the suspicion that she was yet again pregnant. The doctor told her that this was simply menopause - 'the change of life' - and that she was not pregnant. Molly went home unconvinced - though probably also relieved.

A couple of months later, Molly went back to the Coombe and this time marched straight into the office of the doctor who had dealt with her before.

The Change of Life is Kicking

"I have news for you," she announced to him. "The change of life is kicking."

The news of the pregnancy immediately brought fears. Statistically - given Molly's age - there was a very high likelihood that this child would have Down's Syndrome. The state of Molly's health, and her ability to cope with another pregnancy and childbirth, were further cause for concern.

When Molly broke the news of the pregnancy to Barney, they decided that they would start a series of novenas praying for the health of the child. Barney's favourite holy figure was then Blessed (now Saint) Martin de Porres. A picture of this patron saint of the poor hung over Barney's bed: a small red electric lamp before it, its filament shaped like a cross. Barney and Molly promised that the child would be named after Blessed Martin (Martina if the child was a girl) if the child was born healthy.

On Monday August 25th 1952, a somewhat spectacularly healthy baby was born. Weighing in at fourteen pounds, the baby was so big that nurses pretended to walk the newborn Martin up and down the ward. He was also born with a full head of black hair - which later fell out to be replaced by blond hair so light that some people thought he was albino.

With Martin's arrival, there were twelve children at home, ranging from him up to twenty one year old Maureen, in the two bedroom terraced house: the highest number at any one time in the family's history.

"The shakings of the bag," is how next-door neighbour Mrs Donoghue referred to the new arrival. Martin was a shock to the system all round - displacing Ethel from her throne as the youngest, but also coming at a time when life was already getting difficult for

Molly. Not long after the birth, Molly did indeed go through her menopause, and with it entered a depression. Martin was often left for hours in his pram in the front garden. One of Tiny's duties was to be tied to Martin's pram to act as his protector.

"Mammy suffered with her nerves," Betty said. "She wouldn't step outside the door for years, and then when she finally did go out she wouldn't go anywhere without having her rosary beads in her hands. Sometimes Daddy would come down to me and ask me to go to her and help her around the house. She wouldn't talk to neighbours and just kept to herself."

It was a far cry from the days of Molly's youth when she thrived on meeting up with her friends to dance and make music into the night.

Molly had also developed a medical problem that led to her growing what looked like a male Adam's Apple on her throat. The condition, 'goitre', is defined as a 'morbid enlargement of the thyroid gland'. One of its effects is to cause mood swings. More and more often, Barney was the one who would calm things down.

"You know your mother," he would sometimes say to a child who had been slapped or screamed at, "she doesn't really mean it. Leave her and she'll get over it."

The sleeping arrangements were being pushed to the limit in the two bedroom house. Willie can remember a time when four of the brothers slept in one double bed. The oldest brother - Luke, and later Peter - had a single bed in the corner. Barney and the next oldest son shared the other double bed.

"Imagine four kids in a bed - trying to get them to sleep," Willie said.

The Change of Life is Kicking

Bernard recalled a time when the boys were playing instead of settling down to sleep, and Barney had been up twice telling them to be quiet. He warned that if he had to come up again they would be slapped. They started playing again and they heard the rush of footsteps up the stairs. The door burst open.

"Dad stood there, angry," Bernard recalled. "Then he looked at the bunch of us in the middle of our scrap - and he burst out laughing and walked out."

While the younger brothers were having fun, Peter was having a lot of problems in school. He had always been in some way removed from the routine of those around him, and this became more pronounced.

"Sometimes I'd be sitting in class and I'd look out the window and you could see the Dublin Mountains," he said, "and I'd ask to be allowed to go to the toilet and then I'd just walk out of the school towards the mountains and just keep on walking."

"Peter was a very unhappy child," Greta recalled. "I'm sure he never meant to, but he gave Mammy a lot of worry. He would leave for school and Mammy wouldn't know if he had gone to school. With so many children, Mammy wasn't able to keep a close watch on him. Peter was a loner."

He had a history of running away - and when he returned, it would often turn out that he had been staying around Crumlin and would sometimes look in the windows of his home at night.

Ultimately, the authorities decided that he had to be taken into care. He was sent to the Oblate Order's Daingean institution in Kerry. He would spend two years there.

"I remember asking where Peter was," Bernard said, "and being told he had gone to stay with someone else. But we knew it was different. There was something else involved."

Decades later it was discovered that the place Peter was sent to was a living hell of abuse and violence. It became the subject of court cases and a national tribunal. It must have left its mark on him.

In the small house with so many children, accidents could happen. One evening, Martin was parked in his pram beside the door to the scullery while the family sat around the table in the middle of the room. Greta had gone to bring in the pot of tea that was heating on the oven, and as she returned Willie bumped into her, knocking over the pot.

She secured the pot by resting the scalding base on her arm - giving herself a permanent scar to save Martin.

"I suppose anyone would have thought of it because of a baby," Greta said.

It was around this time too that Willie was showing signs of his rebellious nature.

"We lived an awful lot on bread and butter," Willie recalled, "and one time, Mam and Dad decided that they wanted to change over to margarine because margarine was much cheaper than butter. Most of the family accepted it, with one exception - me. I went on hunger strike. I wouldn't eat for two days until they agreed to go back to butter."

Molly said that Barney could still be jealous. Molly would sometimes stand in the back garden talking over the railings with the widowed next door neighbour Mister McGurrell. Or sometimes she would chat with Mister Donoghue on the other side. Barney always became annoyed by this. The Donoghues had six children, but Mister Donoghue was a merchant seaman who basically would be away for most of the year. The couple didn't get along, and when he was around Mrs Donoghue rarely spoke with her husband.

Molly could be fanatical about her housekeeping. One day, she had sent off the family and then immediately set to work putting up new wallpaper in the living room and rearranging all the furniture. By the end of the day the front room was transformed. Barney came home late that evening and was drunk. He turned the key in the door and walked into the livingroom. He halted. It was a common problem that keys fit the halldoors of several houses in the estate.

"Oh I'm sorry Missus," he said, and turned around and left the house.

Molly had to go after him down the path to bring him back in to his newly decorated home.

With families growing up, crowds of youths would gather in different parts of the field in front of the house on Leighlin Road.

"If Mam came out, which wasn't very often, everything would go quiet," Willie recalled. "It meant somebody was in trouble because the boss was out."

"Mammy was a hard woman out of necessity," Kevin said. "She kept life as simple as possible for Dad because he had to work so much. It wasn't a man's job to run the house. Daddy wouldn't lift a cup - men those days didn't do any housework."

All agreed that whatever might have happened during the day would be forgotten about by the time Barney got home - Molly had already dealt out the discipline and it was done with. Another important factor in all this is that Barney was always a frail man and suffered with stomach and ulcer problems. Molly wanted him to have no stress, and so she took it all on herself.

"Mammy was a strong woman," Ethel said. "She had to be. That was how it worked between Mammy and Daddy. They protected each other, and they did anything and everything for the good of their children. Mammy saved Daddy from the daily worries as best she could. Daddy provided for us as best he could. That was life then. The women took care of the children, the house, and the discipline. The men went off to work."

"I think as a family, the Duffys were seen as being big - but also clean and respectable," Willie recalled. "Even though we were a big family and were poor, Mam kept us all clean. You'd see some other kids who were wearing the same clothes for months at a time."

The many children around in Crumlin brought another kind of co-operation.

"It was usual for people to pass Confirmation or Communion clothes over the railing from one family to the next," Brigid said. She also recalled a time when the nuns in her school would give her bundles of clothes to bring home for her brothers and sisters. From time to time in the year also - especially at Christmas - Kennedy's Bakery would deliver a fresh loaf to every child in the school. This meant that five Duffy children would come down Leighlin Road, each with a loaf of bread under his or her arm.

"When we got Christmas toys," Bernard said, "we knew they weren't new."

Then again, music and life always filled the house. Betty having married and left, the job of taking care of the younger children had passed on to Maureen, Breda and Greta. Ethel has a distinct memory of Breda, one Christmas Eve, sitting her on the board over the bath

The Change of Life is Kicking

and singing Christmas songs to her while she was peeling potatoes and slicing vegetables. Greta was always singing too.

Ethel recalled that, despite the workload involved in taking care of all the children and all the preparations needed around Christmas time, Molly would always clear out the fireplace on the night of Christmas Eve so the children could see that Santa would be able to come down the chimney.

Bernard, Paddy, Martin and Kevin

In the early Fifties, there were seven children under the age of fourteen running around the little house. By then, the home had a third-in-command in the form of eldest brother Luke, and by then he also had begun to use the complaint that would become his nickname; 'shut the door!'. He was infuriated by the kids coming in and out and always leaving doors open. Luke was known for a few forms of intolerance. Sniffling was another activity that got him angered.

"'Stop breathing' is all he was short of saying," Kevin recalled.

Luke enjoyed gambling, and on the field in front of the houses there would be what were called 'gambling schools' - large groups of teenagers and young men playing pitch and toss.

"You were paid on Friday," Luke recalled, "and in the evening there would be four or five schools. You played the game with two ha'pennies, if it was two heads you won, if it was two tails you lost, if it was one of each you just threw again. You bet on your throw, and the men looking on would either back with or against you. After a couple of hours, a school would close because one or two fellas had won all the money and so those people would join another school. This would go on until finally all the fellas who had won would start gambling together - it would be Saturday by the time that came around.

"Always, too, there would be a fella - usually the toughest of the group - who would be controlling the game. He wouldn't make any bets himself, but he would be pushing people back to keep room and he might have a big leather belt and swing it to make sure there was a big enough circle for the game. At this stage, too, there were about a hundred people around but only a dozen of them backing money because all the rest had lost theirs.

"Every so often - no matter that this big fella was there - if there were enough people without money, they'd want a bit back. Maybe once a month or so, someone from the back would shout out DIVE! and

The Change of Life is Kicking

everyone would dive at the money on the ground. There were bodies flying everywhere and that money was gone - it didn't matter who owned it."

It happened to Luke - but he said it was part of the territory. It certainly didn't put him off gambling.

"If the money held out and your luck held out," he said, "you could be tossing coins on Friday night and on Saturday, and then if your money was still holding out you could be playing cards under lamplight and next thing you know it's six o'clock on Sunday morning and you'd walk down to Mount Argus for first Mass. If you had a good weekend, you might be going home with fifteen or twenty pound that you'd won - which back then was a hell of a lot of money."

"Luke was always considered a bit of a dark horse by the other guys on the street," Willie recalled. "He didn't pal around all that much with the local guys. He tended to go off and do his own thing. He would gamble out on the field, but while the other guys would go off and do something together, he wouldn't. He was respected as a guy who could take care of himself."

The large field at the back of the houses - although it was usually wild and overgrown - was often used by the more serious gamblers who didn't want to be bothered by kids looking on.

Barney would occasionally also join in this gambling on the field, but above all he enjoyed playing cards at home on a Sunday afternoon. These games became a great tradition, especially as the boyfriends of the daughters started swelling the ranks of players. Barney's brother Peter was a regular at the table. There was also a dart board in the living room, and Barney loved to play that too.

Barney and Molly

In the summer of 1953, Greta and her boyfriend Tom Carroll headed off for a cycling holiday in England that would lead them to London. Before they went, Molly asked Greta to see if she could make contact with Luke Dowdall - Molly had lost contact with her brother, whose marriage had by then broken down. The only clue Molly could offer was that Luke Dowdall worked in one of the chain of the many Lyons Tea Rooms in London.

When Greta and Tom finally reached London, Greta felt that she should at least make some gesture for her mother's sake. She had come out from a tube station and saw a Lyon's Corner House café. She saw a doorman there and approached him.

"Excuse me," she said to him. "Could you tell me how I could find out if a Luke Dowdall works in one of these cafés."

"Luke Dowdall," the man repeated.

"Yes," Greta said. "My Mammy is his sister."

"Do you know where he is?" the man asked.

"I haven't a clue," Greta said.

"You're talking to him."

Unlike his brother Willie Dowdall, Luke Dowdall had no gift for or interest in music. He was a handsome man with a fine head of black hair and a charming smile. He did not always enjoy good health and so could only do light work, but there are no details of what he suffered from. Luke Dowdall had been in the British Army and he had served in the Home Guard in London during the Second World War. His ex-wife, Victoria, was not Irish. They had two sons together. Given the rarity of failed marriages in those times, it is somehow unusual that Mother and Father Dowdall's only two sons both had failed marriages.

The Change of Life is Kicking

When Tom and Greta found Luke Dowdall by this amazing coincidence, he brought them for a meal. It was the start of regaining some contact with his family. The connection, however, was not destined to work out very well. Luke Dowdall later moved back to Dublin and was soon confronted with financial hardships.

Later in 1953, Greta split up from Tom Carroll. When Tom and Greta split, he went to England to work and to gain more experience in his trade. Greta later began dating her next door neighbour - John McGurrell. Greta's brother Luke, meanwhile, had started dating a young local woman named Angela Hughes.

Breda was dating, and was very fond of Ceili dancing. She frequently went to the Ierne Ballroom on Parnell Street. Greta recalled that one boyfriend of Breda's, a young man named Matt Doran, was from Swords on the Northside of Dublin and was a farmer.

"He was very nice and good looking," Greta recalled, "but I always remembered he had a pin holding up his trousers."

Greta fondly recalled one time when her sister Breda showed the level of co-operation and support there was in the family.

"Breda had a beautiful blouse that she had bought in Cassidy's," Greta said, "and I asked her if I could borrow it. Breda said I could. So I ironed it - and the whole face of the iron came off the front of the blouse. She never complained. If it was me I'd probably have gone hysterical. But she never complained. 'what's done is done,' is all she said."

Greta loved ballroom dancing - she went often to the Olympic Ballroom, and loved the foxtrot and waltzes. The love of music and dancing had passed

Barney and Molly

from Molly to her children. They weren't dancing at the crossroads, but romance was in the air for Barney and Molly's children as one by one they crossed the threshold into adulthood. In the decade to come, weddings would be an almost annual event in the family.

Molly and Betty at 147

Workers and Children

Molly was devoted to the workers in the family and did everything for them - they were the lifeblood for the survival of the family and she served them in every way she could. As each family member came home from work, Molly would meet them at the door and take their bikes to bring out to the bike shed in the back garden while they took their coats off and prepared to eat the dinner Molly had prepared for them.

"There was a hierarchy at the dinner table," Peter recalled. "Whoever was working got their dinner first and only they sat at the table - everyone else waited. If you lost your job, you also lost your place at the table."

The hierarchy worked in other ways.

"Luke was bringing in money so he was the big guy," Willie recalled. "So if he wanted to sit in that chair - guess what - you got up and he sat in that chair." Martin remembered that he, as the youngest, almost always sat on the floor.

"It took two sittings to have a meal," Willie recalled, "and the whole place was a nightmare with kids running around. The best day was Friday, because everyone was paid and it was Mam's day off from cooking and we all got fish and chips."

Luke had his say in this, too. Luke didn't like fish and chips. So while the others could have their fish and chips, Molly made him a favourite treat of his own; rice pudding with jam.

"I was the only one who ever had it," Luke said, "and Mam made it specially in a dish for me."

Both Greta and Brigid recalled the extent to which Molly took special care of Luke and pandered to his tastes.

"The girls got what was coming for their dinner," Greta recalled, "but when Luke came in, Mammy would say 'ah Luke, what would you like to eat?'"

"He'd often tell her before he went out what he wanted to have on the table when he came home," Brigid added.

If Luke didn't like the smell of the dinner as he was walking up the path to the house, he'd throw his bike under the front windowsill in annoyance.

Once, Willie nearly choked on a potato. Molly was setting food on the table when a knock came to the door. Willie saw his chance. He grabbed a potato out of the pot and popped it in his mouth - but it was steaming hot and lodged in his throat. He was trying to fan his mouth and cough the potato out, wailing. Molly returned and thought he was acting like the Indians in the cowboy films.

"Don't you be playing games around me when I'm trying to get up the dinner," Molly said to him, giving him a clout. Then it dawned on her what was happening and she helped him.

While the workers were sitting for their meal at the table in the front room, the non-workers (the children) sat in the scullery eating theirs. They could sometimes get out of control - taunting each other and messing. Brigid, however, always had one last line of defence.

"If you don't leave me alone," she'd say, "I'm going to get you into trouble."

All Brigid had to do was stand back from the table and call out 'oh me eye me eye'.

"Daddy would run in battering them," Brigid recalled with a laugh. "It was the only time I saw Daddy like that - he had skin and hair flying. So that was always my trick - 'me eye'." By the time she was fourteen, however, Brigid finally completely recovered from her eye problem and could see properly without glasses. Happily, too, the headaches and vomiting were a thing of the past.

"Mam was always working," Bernard recalled. "I distinctly remember her getting a cramp in her arm from slicing bread. When I got home from school at lunchtime I would quickly get something to eat and then run down to the bakers to pick up a load of Vienna rolls for her, then rush back to school. That was my job every day."

There were plenty of jobs to be delegated - the boys would be sent to the shops, and the girls had chores when they got home from school.

"I remember one time I lost a ha'penny on my way back from the shops," Kevin said, "I'd been to Johnson Mooney and O'Brien's bakers for bread. I was beaten by Mammy, and I had to go back and find it. I was at an age where I had those kind of jobs to do that the ones who were working no longer had to do."

The majority of the work rested on Molly's shoulders. Although everyone went to full time work as soon as possible after completing their primary education - and would have already been doing part time jobs before that - Molly was the hardest physical labourer in the family.

Molly's daily routine was a relentless round of work to keep her husband and twelve children fed, clean and healthy in a spotless home. She would make breakfast for everyone, and would also prepare a packed lunch for each of the workers. When that was done, she would set about cleaning the house and washing the clothes. She would make a lunch for the boys coming home on their break from school.

"I remember times coming home from school," Ethel said, "and Mammy would still be at the sink washing clothes since morning time. And yet another day you might come home from school and find the place painted and papered. I don't know where she got her strength and energy from."

In the afternoons, Molly's attention would turn to shopping and then she would set to work preparing a meal for fourteen every evening. She would peel a stone of potatoes every day.

"One meal I remember was chicken stew," Brigid said. "She would get three chickens that went into a huge pot that took over most of the top of the cooker."

In the evening time, Molly's attention would turn to the next cleaning job; her children. The girls all had long hair that Molly would brush thoroughly every night. In the mornings, she would then tie the girls' hair back in plaits or pigtails.

"She'd tie our hair back so tight," Brigid said, "we'd look like we were Chinese."

Molly paid great care and attention to Barney. In the mornings, she would make him an egg flip - raw egg, warm milk and sugar - with his breakfast as it was good for his delicate stomach. She would also have bought cigarettes from Maher's shop across the field to put in his pocket and would make his lunch. He'd go out to work in the morning not knowing what was in his lunch. Molly simply put it in his pocket. Sometimes, in winter, Molly would even give him a small 'nip' of whiskey to heat him up at the start of the day. In the evenings, she'd take the bike from him at the door and put it in the shed while he had a wash. The dinner would be on the table for him when he was ready to sit down to it.

"Jaysus Molly," he'd sometimes say, "it's so hot, it'd scald a Protestant."

"The one thing that I ever saw annoying Daddy was if his dinner wasn't ready," Kevin said. "I always remember how he'd come in from work, wash himself, and then sit to eat. He would expect his dinner to be on the table."

There was a flip side to this, however. One time, Barney had come home late having stayed too long in the pub. Molly had kept his dinner warm, on a plate over a simmering pot of water on the oven. Barney sat down to eat his dinner.

"Molly," he said to her, "the dinner is too hot."

"Hot!" Molly replied. "Hot is it! I'll cool it for ya!"

She grabbed the plate of food and threw it out into the back garden. Later, she sent one of the kids out to find out if the plate was still in one piece.

Barney, as always, worked long hours. Bernard recalled how the kids would wait until Barney came home - around eight or nine in the evening.

"He would sit down to have his dinner and we'd all be sitting round him. And he'd wind up giving us each a bit of his food. It was only later looking back I realised - no wonder he was thin. He might give us most of his food."

Barney would then go and sit in his chair in the corner beside the fireplace and promptly fall asleep.

"There was a clump of hair at the back of his head that would stand up," Bernard recalled, "and Greta in particular was always wetting it and trying to get it to lie down. It would lie down for a few minutes, and then spring back up again."

The system with income in the house remained straightforward; everyone - including Barney - handed their pay packet to Molly. She would then hand them back their weekly allowance.

"All his life, Daddy had brought his pay packet home and handed it to Mammy," Kevin said. "So what he had was whatever Mam could afford to give him. And that sometimes was just a few shillings. She never gave him the money for Saturday on Friday. It was one day at a time for his own good."

Food was always basic. A roast beef set on the table on Sunday was the highlight. This meat was used in sandwiches the next morning and the last cuts of it were eaten for Monday's dinner. Tuesday was likely to be a stew - with the bones of the beef as the meat content. Wednesday and Thursday the options were likely to be some cheap cut of meat such as heart or tongue or pigs feet or coddle (sausages in soup). Friday was fish. Saturday was usually lamb chops. Potatoes were a constant. There would always be one or two vegetables - usually cauliflower, cabbage, peas or carrots.

Mrs Nugent, who lived on Kells Road, came around on Wednesdays and Fridays selling fish. She came pushing a pram with the boxes of fish and a bread board across the pram. She would stand outside 147 and shout 'Duffy! Do you want fish today!' Molly would come out with a big plate to buy fish.

There was a Father Paul Mary, a priest from Mount Argus, who often visited the home. He would sometimes sit out on the field in front of the houses to play cards with the lads. He also sometimes ate with the family.

"If I had heart on, or pigs feet," Molly said, "he'd be in looking for a bit of it."

One time, Molly called on the priest's help for a strange problem - she believed part of the house was haunted. The area under the stairs made a small storage room in the living room that was called 'the coal house'. This had a door with small air holes. Sometimes, things would be thrown out through these holes.

"I remember times we were all sitting around the fire," Brigid said, "and things started getting thrown out those small holes. We'd look around at who was there - to see if someone was missing who might be up to these antics. But no one was missing. Once, Luke went over to the door, and he got a bang on the head from something thrown out."

Father Paul Mary blessed the house and there was no further trouble.

"I remember times when Mammy wouldn't go to bed on a Saturday night," Greta said, "because you had to be spotless on Sunday. I remember working with girls who said to me 'are you one of the Duffys that have all the brothers that always have snow white shirts?' Mammy was a very hard worker."

"I always remember that in school if an Inspector came around or a priest visited the class," Brigid said, "it would always be one of us who would be brought to the top of the class to show how clean and neat we were."

Given this famous cleanliness, it is astonishing that it was only in the mid Fifties, after almost thirty years of raising children, that Molly got her first washing machine. And this was not a model you loaded up, switched on and forgot about. First a hose had to be attached to the tap and the machine filled up, then this water was heated by the machine, then you loaded the washing and the washing powder. The machine then went into action with its churn back and forth washing the clothes. There was a ringer at the back of the machine and you rolled the wet, washed clothes through this. The washing was then rinsed in the sink in cold water to get the soap out of it, and then again put through the ringer to get it dry enough to hang them out on the washing line.

Before this development, everything had been washed by hand. Clothes were cleaned in the deep 'Belfast sink' in the scullery and a glass scrubbing board. Sunlight Soap was rubbed into the clothes, and then the clothes were scrubbed against the board.

"Mam usually left me the job of doing the socks," Brigid recalled. "I'd be scrubbing them with my fists on the scrubbing board. There were times when the house smelt like a laundry - there was so much washing."

One thing Martin still shudders to remember is how Molly would boil up a pot of dirty handkerchiefs. It was the most hygienic way to clean them: but an absolutely disgusting sight.

Workers and Children

One thing the house couldn't cope with was the bed sheets - given there were so many beds in the house. This was costly, however, and Molly had a system of rotating the sheets so that the bottom sheets only were given to the laundry man who came around, and what had been the top sheet would be used on the bottom and a fresh top sheet put on the beds.

Sometimes, the pressure to keep things clean meant that Molly would start to do some washing on Sunday but Barney would absolutely forbid it.

Weekends at home were a time for fun and industriousness. Everyone had jobs to do in Molly's regime of keeping the home - and everyone in it - clean.

"I remember being pushed under the beds with a small hand brush to clean there," Brigid recalled.

"And when Mam got new beds that were lower, I would be squeezed in under the beds," Ethel, five years younger, added. "Then you were squeezed back under the bed with a tin of polish to put a shine on the floor."

Every detail was kept spic and span. Even the rods holding down the carpet on the stairs would be removed and their brass tips polished with Brasso.

Whitening runners and putting them on the window ledge to dry was another weekly job. Ethel remembered Bernard doing her runners - he was the most experienced. The girls' sandals would be polished with red 'ox blood' polish.

On Saturday nights the children got their cod liver oil and their hair would be fine-combed to check for lice or nits.

"There was a big tin bath," Brigid recalled, "and I can remember Breda bathing us all in it on a Saturday night. Then you'd be put into your clean nightdress and your clean clothes for Sunday would be set out - and that'd be you ready for bed."

Once a month the children were given a tea called 'Sennaleaves' for their bowels and they would be queuing up for the toilet.

Sunday tea time was another big event as family and friends would gather. The Sunday tea - with cakes and biscuits - was a major treat. Though as always, the children had to wait until the adults had eaten.

"I always remember Betty's husband Patsy," Bernard said. "He was a mechanic and he'd always arrive in different cars he was working on and he always looked as if he'd just climbed out from under an engine. It seemed like his hands were covered in black grease. He also had a particular habit of grinding his teeth, and as a kid I used to try impersonating him."

Barney and Molly were on a constant treadmill of work and self-sacrifice. But they were devoted to their family and they were devoted to each other. Greta recalled a time when Barney came home and gave Molly a brooch.

"To me it was as if it was set with real diamonds and rubies, and that's how much she treasured it too. He wasn't the kind of man who would go in to a shop to buy something like that, but he went in and bought it himself and that alone made it special. Mammy loved it."

With Maureen being at the Royal, Barney and Molly would go there most Saturday nights for the show. It was a well-earned break from their huge workload keeping their big family going, and it meant that for the first time since the early days of the marriage Molly was getting out regularly.

Workers and Children

Bernard also remembered being taken along to see Roy Rogers and his wonder horse Trigger - who could do simple addition with the stomping of his hoof.

Peter, meanwhile, was back from his time in the home in Kerry. He had, however, become an even darker soul. One time, he was left in charge of the children when Molly and Barney went out. They came back unexpectedly early to find Willie tied to a chair and with an imprint of a fist on his forehead. Willie and Peter both said they were playing - and Barney and Molly decided to leave it at that. What they didn't know was that on another occasion when Peter was left in charge, he had punched Willie unconscious. He had stood Willie against a wall and wanted to see how hard he could punch him - but the punch also slammed Willie's head against the wall. Peter frantically tried to get Willie to regain consciousness before their parents came home.

"We always swore that when we got older we'd beat the crap out of him," Kevin joked about Peter.

Maureen regularly brought people home from the Royal, adding to the life of the house. At the celebration of her twenty first birthday, 147 was packed out with people from the Royal. It suited Maureen's warm and outgoing nature to have so many friends around her.

Once, there was a competition in the Royal in which couples got up on stage and sang together. Barney and Molly took part and made their way through, over a number of weeks, to the final. The prize was a huge Christmas hamper. Barney had become ill, but still got out of his sick bed to go with Molly. Up on stage, they sang 'My Blue Heaven'; 'just Molly and me, and baby makes three, we're living in my blue heaven...'

They won first prize. Ethel and Brigid remembered the huge tins of biscuits and crisps and the lemonade.

In due course, Maureen and Austin decided to get engaged. They took the bold step at the time of not telling anyone and simply going out and getting the ring. They then showed up at Leighlin Road and announced that they were engaged. Molly's sister Delia was there when they made the announcement.

"Come out here you," Delia said to Austin, and brought him into the scullery. She gave him a dressing down.

"How dare you go out and get engaged without telling her Mam and Dad or without asking permission."

Maureen and Austin Wedding

Maureen married Austin on June 28th 1954. The wedding party was held in 147 - the catering being handled by the parents of Luke's girlfriend Angela Hughes. The popularity of Maureen and Austin pushed the living space in Leighlin Road past its limits.

"The house was completely packed out," Austin recalled. "Especially with the Royalettes. I remember I ended up with a piece of wedding cake and a cup of tea sitting on the bottom step of the stairs in the hall."

There are many telling details in the photographs from the wedding. Not least is to see that Molly by now was sporting false teeth after what may have been close to two decades without teeth. She was certainly looking healthier than in the photographs at Betty's wedding eight years earlier.

Dublin Corporation had a raffle for newly weds, and Austin and Maureen won the key to a maisonette flat in Milltown. Fortune was smiling on their new married life. Maureen left the Theatre Royal, as it was practically unheard of for women to keep working after getting married, but later she would go back to work again.

Perhaps as a result of the cramped conditions for Maureen's wedding party, Barney and Molly decided on a change to the layout of their home. The door from the front room to the scullery was in the middle of the wall and this, combined with the fact that the door to the back garden and toilet opened inwards, created a lot of wasted space in a home that was already crowded. They decided to move the door down to beside the 'coal house' - the storage space under the stairs. This freed up more working space in the scullery,

But there was one unanticipated consequence of this.

"Daddy's chair was always in the corner by the coal house," Luke recalled, "but with the door moved - he didn't know where to sit." Furniture was rearranged so that Barney's chair moved into the other corner, just beside the fireplace.

"It was as bad as the time I moved his coat hanger from inside the front door to inside the coal house," Luke recalled. "I hardly heard the end of that from him."

In January 1955 Paddy, having turned fifteen, quit school without completing his last year in order to start full time work. He was soon working in the local cinema, the Bower on Sundrive Road, as an usher. His brother Willie, always somehow following suit, got a job in the city centre's Carlton Cinema also as an usher - taking particular joy in his uniform and the small pill box hat that was part of the outfit. Willie always loved style.

Bernard remembered his turns at bringing food over to Mother and Father Dowdall - aside from the money and provisions she would send them, Molly would also make a Sunday meal for them.

"Father Dowdall was very anti-British," Bernard said. "He would often tell me about the Black and Tans and the things they did."

"I was sent to them every Saturday," Brigid recalled, "with their rent money wrapped up, and a pound of round steak, a pound of butter, a half pound of tea, a large sliced pan, and tobacco for Father Dowdall. They were living in one room. They had two white enamel buckets and no running water, so I'd go down to the back yard to fill up the buckets with fresh water for them. On Sunday I'd be sent again with their cooked dinner carried in a big bowl wrapped up to keep the food warm."

Mother Dowdall became more eccentric in her money-sparing ways. There were times when she would stay in bed all day to save the cost of lighting a fire.

Workers and Children

If Mother Dowdall wasn't always the most endearing of souls, Ethel remembered Father Dowdall as the perfect grandfather. "What more could you want," she said, "than a grandfather with snow white hair and a wooden leg."

Molly's father died on March 25th 1955. There was an unusual twist to the tragedy. The elderly couple had both taken ill, and Mother Dowdall was so ill that she was anointed - given last rites - in bed at home. She had been in bad health for years, and there was a sense of acceptance when death seemed close for her. Then Father Dowdall contracted bronchitis and became even more ill. He had to take to the bed instead.

A Garda car came to 147 late in the evening to break the news to Molly that both her parents were seriously ill. The buses were no longer running, and the Gardai brought Molly - who took her son Willie along to help - over to her parents.

Maureen was with the family the next day as the old man lay dying. Willie Dowdall, still living in the flat across the hall from his parents, asked her to go into Clery's shop in town to buy black ties and the black star patches traditionally worn on the left arm of the jackets of those in bereavement.

"I was afraid Father Dowdall would die in the hour I'd be away," Maureen recalled, "and I said to him 'hang on old man'. I went into town and got back. Within ten minutes I heard the deep sigh as he gave up his last breath."

Father Dowdall had been battling bronchitis for two weeks when his heart gave way. He died at home of myocardial failure. He was seventy two years old. His son Willie signed as witness for the death certificate. Molly was deeply upset by her father's death. She was very close to him, and he was a far more affectionate person than Mother Dowdall.

After Father Dowdall died, his son Luke came back from England. Luke Dowdall, however, had come for one reason; he wanted the money he knew his mother hoarded. Luke had stayed overnight with Maureen and Austin in Milltown, and left early next morning.

Later that day, Maureen was contacted with the news that Mother Dowdall's home had been ransacked. It transpired that Luke had tried to find where his mother hid her money.

"My mother was a miser," Molly said. "She had a knitted waistcoat with four pockets that she kept money in, and she had a money belt as well. Luke took all the money. Delia and I went up to Pembroke Street. We found Luke there unconscious drunk. Me and Delia threw a bucket of water over him lying on the bed and then we beat him. We never saw him again after that."

Luke Dowdall returned to London.

In the search for regular work, Maureen and Austin emigrated to England in 1955. After a while they moved to a flat at Vauxhall Bridge where they lived for some time. Austin worked as a 'clippie' - a bus conductor. They became the first in the family to make a move that in the coming years would be the only solution for many of the younger ones. In the late Fifties, Dev's Ireland couldn't cope with all those children his loyal Catholic population was producing in such vast quantities. Barney and Molly's children would be part of an exodus of this Irish generation in search of work.

The Scattering Begins

147 Leighlin Road teemed with life. There were eleven children ranging from child Martin to adults Breda and Luke living under Barney and Molly's care in the two-bedroom terraced house. Within the clan there were sub-groups of friends - like Kevin and Bernard, or Willie and Paddy. Many of the schoolchildren already had part time jobs, and everyone was playing their part in the running of the home. Most important, however, was that there was as much fun as work. The home teemed with intelligence, creativity, and industry.

"Saturday afternoons we all had our jobs," Ethel recalled, "but nine times out of ten it would turn into a party. We'd have our dinner listening to the 'Walton's' sponsored radio show, presented by Leo Maguire. He always said 'if you feel like singing, do sing an Irish song'. Later in the evening was the 'Din Joe' show. Then Peter would start playing the piano, and everyone would take their turn to sing."

Ethel recalled how Barney particularly enjoyed radio programmes, even listening regularly to the shipping forecast from the BBC Home Service. Why Barney would want to know the conditions for fishermen and sea-farers off the shores of Ireland and the United Kingdom is unclear, but he was always an avid gatherer of information.

"I remember on Sunday evenings sitting around the fire with Daddy listening to a radio programme of ghost stories," Ethel said. The show was presented by Val Vousden. "Daddy would wind us up even more. He'd frighten the life out of us."

For Bernard, the highlight of radio listening was the pop music on Radio Luxembourg.

"During the evenings we'd try to tune it in," he recalled, "and it'd fade away and come back. You'd be playing with the knob and swearing at the radio as the signal faded and came back. It was where we heard Elvis Presley, Little Richard and the others - it was the only station playing that music. Sunday nights they played the Top Twenty."

Bernard, by then, was becoming aware not just of rock 'n' roll, but of girls.

"Sometimes Bernard would leave me stuck up on the railings at the back of the house," Kevin said, "because he wanted to go off chatting up the girls and I was too young and he didn't want me with him."

Crumlin was awash with hormones as rakes of boys and girls reached their teens. Kevin fancied two local girls - Noleen Hennessy and Patricia Conway.

Kevin was always on the go. He would run errands for the older brothers and sisters in return for a penny here and there. He would join the queue at the Bower cinema on Sundrive Road and hold a place for Willie who would then arrive and tip him a penny or two. On another occasion, however, Kevin was with some pals who were trying to bunk into the cinema by climbing over a metal fence. His hand caught and he got a massive rip from his wrist to the top of a finger.

The Scattering Begins

Some of Molly's mercurial ways were easing off. One time, Ethel bent the rules by spending her bus money on sweets and walking home from the Coombe school. She therefore arrived home late. When she walked in the door, Molly started giving out and throwing things at her that were within reach.

"I hid behind a chair," Ethel recalled, "and she had thrown shoes and things. Then the only thing left in her reach was a big - and valuable - Waterford Crystal bowl. She picked it up. I thought 'Oh my god, I'm finished'."

"I was watching," Brigid said. "I couldn't believe it."

"Then Mammy said 'you're not worth it' and put the bowl back down," Ethel recalled. "I said to myself 'thank you, God'."

Not that this would stop the children from provoking Molly. They knew what she was like - but they did not live in fear of her. Ethel recalled a time when she gave back cheek to Molly and then ran up to the front bedroom and blocked herself behind the two double beds there so that Molly couldn't reach her. Molly threw shoes at her as Ethel carried on taunting until Molly finally gave up.

Kevin and Bernard also regularly thwarted Molly. They would be sent to bed and then carry on playing and messing for an hour and more. Molly would shout up the stairs at them to go asleep, but soon she'd hear them running around in the bedroom again.

There were wooden rods holding in the carpet on the stairs, and finally Molly would go up to Kevin and Bernard and lift out one of these rods to hit them. The thing is - Kevin and Bernard would hear this happening.

They'd crawl under the covers and shield themselves with the pillows, so that Molly would come in and roar at them and hit them with the rod and they'd be crying out 'oh ow' and under the covers they'd be trying not to laugh.

"In the end she caught them," Ethel said, "because she'd be going down the stairs and she'd hear them laughing and she'd run up saying 'so yiz want more'. Finally she realised."

One thing that Barney would never put up with was if the children said anything against Molly. Brigid recalled a time when her Uncle Peter and Aunt Mary had come to visit 147. Meanwhile, Molly had gone out because a neighbour had taken away a ball that had gone into their garden. This started to develop into an argument. Brigid, looking out the window at this, said "oh look, Mammy's out there having a big row."

"Up that stairs to bed!" Barney shouted at her. At the foot of the stairs in the hall, Brigid made the mistake of pausing. What became a legendary knack of Barney's then ensued: a kick in the pants that could launch a kid at least half way up the stairs.

"I think I landed up on the top step," Brigid said. "It was the only time he ever hit me. He was furious with me for thinking it was funny to see Mammy out on the road having a row."

For all the chaos and work at home, Barney and Molly were a jolly couple who very rarely argued. In general among the children, also, there was little more than the normal tiffs. But the two eldest sons, Luke and Peter, were a different matter. They were far stricter with the younger ones than Molly - and certainly Barney - and Ethel and Brigid recall how Luke and Peter were the ones who were constantly giving out to them. No one, however, questioned Barney's authority. And one time, Peter crossed an absolutely forbidden line.

"Peter had hit Greta," Brigid said, "and hitting a woman was one thing Daddy would not stand for. It had happened on a Saturday night when Mammy and Daddy were out, and Barney found out about it on Sunday evening. He decided to do nothing about it at that time. Then, on Monday evening, he got home from work and Peter was home. Daddy hung his coat up on the back of the scullery door, then rolled up his shirt sleeves and stood in front of Peter."

"You and I have something to sort out," Barney said to Peter. "I think you know what I'm talking about."

Peter said nothing, looking around and not knowing what to do.

"Come on," Barney insisted. "We'll deal with it out in the back yard. If you want to hit anybody, try and hit me."

Barney was always a slight man. Brigid looked at the two men and thought 'if Peter hits him he'll kill him'.

"I don't want to go out," Peter said to his father. Barney pushed him out to the back yard.

"I'm not going to hit you," Peter said.

"Well I'm going to hit you," Barney replied, and slapped him a few times.

Peter wouldn't raise his hands to his father.

In 1956, Molly's financial wizardry brought a new gadget into the house - a television. The Duffys were the first family in the area to get one. The founding of an Irish national television station was a long way off, so the tall aerial on the chimney struggled to pick up signals from the two British stations.

"The first programme we saw on the television was 'the 6-5 Special' - a pop music programme," Brigid recalled.

"Often, all you'd see was some kind of grey mush that looked like it might be something," Bernard recalled. "But I remember one time I was alone at home and there was a comedy programme on and I was laughing. And I suddenly halted and realised how strange it was. Later, I asked Dad if it was weird to sit on your own laughing."

"What do you mean?" Barney asked him.

"I was on my own laughing at television," Bernard said.

Barney looked at him and said "no no - that's fine."

There was one absolute rule about television that held fast. At the end of their broadcasts, the British channels would play the English national anthem. Barney would instantly have it switched off.

"Get rid of that," he'd bark.

Molly's reputation was such that one time Kevin was at the television set trying to get better reception when he got an electric shock. He spun around to Molly and shouted "What did you hit me for - I didn't do anything!"

Greta was very religious and got the nickname of 'the nun'. This was also in part because she often dressed in black and was always going to Mass. Greta would kneel at the side of the bed for a half hour every night, saying her prayers in a low whisper and thumping her chest - 'oh clement, oh loving, oh sweet Virgin Mary...'

The Scattering Begins

"Are ya finished," Molly would finally snap in exasperation, and then Greta would get into bed.

Luke had asked Angela Hughes to get engaged but she said she didn't want to. Luke, always unhappy about the work situation in Dublin, decided to end the relationship and take his chances finding work and making a new life in London. When he told Angela his plans, she asked if he would stay in Dublin were they to get engaged, but Luke had made up his mind.

"It was a condition too many," Luke said. In July 1956, he emigrated to London.

"It wasn't just that work was scarce in Ireland," he said. "Most of it was also seasonal - so you might only be hired for six months at some factory. A lot of factories had their regulars and then took on other workers on a casual basis."

He first stayed with Maureen and Austin, and then got a flat with a few other Dublin men that he knew. He lived in Victoria, in the centre of London.

Luke renewed contact with his uncle and namesake, Luke Dowdall. At this time in London, Luke Dowdall was sharing a one room flat with a couple who apparently were unmarried but possibly were in a relationship - the man was ten years younger than Luke Dowdall and the woman ten years older. "I met Uncle Luke quite a bit, and even got him a job in the first place I worked." The two Lukes were working in a shop that rented out a vast assortment of costumes and props to film production companies. The firm was called Axford and Son on Vauxhall Bridge Road. "Our job was to show people around the different things we had that matched whatever period they were making their film about."

Luke remembered being with his uncle in the shop when he heard the radio report about Irish runner Ronnie Delaney having won the gold medal in the 1500m race at the 1956 Olympic Games in Melbourne, Australia. Back in Dublin, someone who had heard this news with huge enthusiasm was the family's athlete Bernard.

"Dad was really interested," Bernard said. "Ronnie Delaney was already a hero in Ireland. We listened to the race live on the radio. We could hear the screams and cheers of the crowd. But Dad was always a fan of big sports events - especially boxing. He was a fan of Rocky Marciano and I remember many times Dad coming up to wake me because I wanted to sit and listen with him in the middle of the night to some fight broadcast live from America."

With Luke gone, Peter had been promoted to the single bed, and Bernard recalled a particular incident about Peter and this new arrangement. There was a wardrobe between the single bed and the double bed where the small boys slept. One morning, the mirrored door of this wardrobe had opened and when Peter sat up he saw his own reflection. He cried out in fright. Bernard and Kevin hid under the sheets trying not to let him hear their laughter.

The economy of the Irish Republic wasn't doing well. The population was growing - and so was unemployment. There had often been demonstrations on the street of Dublin by the unemployed. The rest of Europe was growing economically at a rate five time faster than that of Ireland, and emigration was at its highest since its days as a colony of England. These were not good times to be reaching a working age, and one marriage in the family was to prove important for the young Duffy men: Gerry Kinsella was going to have a big impact on the lives of the Duffy brothers.

Breda was always very busy with house chores and with her social life. She was famous for over-dressing when she went out.

"She'd be going to a dance, and you'd think it was a ball," Brigid remembered.

Breda loved parties. Her boyfriend, Gerry Kinsella, was in a cyclist group and Breda would often invite them over for a party. Gerry was another new arrival to the clan who loved the life and warmth. He called Molly 'Mother Moll'. He was also another close neighbour marrying into the family - he had grown up on Monasterboice Road, a road in view of 147.

Bernard remembered that Gerry took an interest in his athletics, and would often go to support him at races.

Bernard also recalled a time when his uncle Amby Duffy was with him at an event at which Bernard won several trophies.

"He collected me at the school," Bernard said, "and I had a load of cups and trophies and a fruit bowl and a sugar bowl and Amby picked me up and sat me on the crossbar of his bike and cycled me home." What a fine image Bernard must have made, on the crossbar clutching his armful of trophies as he made his triumphal return to 147.

Breda and Gerry decided to get married. Breda's hen party was held in 147. This being a woman's-only event, Barney and all the brothers had been ordered out of the house. Barney had been delayed a little, and as a group of women from Cassidy's arrived they were going upstairs to put their coats away as Barney was coming downstairs to leave. When the girls came back down to Breda, they all said 'who was that man coming down the stairs - he's gorgeous.'

"Will you stop it!" Breda said to them, "that's my Da!"

Breda and Gerry married in December 1956. There were ten couples on the altar that day. The wedding party was celebrated in a marquee built in the back garden of the Kinsella home on Monasterboice Road. The catering for the event was done by the parents of Luke's ex-girlfriend Angela Hughes.

Breda and Gerry moved to London shortly after marrying. They lived in Croydon - which would become a home away from home for other Duffys to come. Indeed, as Luke had been like a second father in the household in Crumlin, Breda became like the English mother to the family as one brother after another emigrated to London and was taken under the wing of Gerry and Breda.

Maureen and Austin, living in London, were starting their family. Their first baby was due in February 1957. This happy and winning couple were about to enter the next phase of their lives - parenthood. Then tragedy struck. It was discovered that the child Maureen was carrying had died.

Terrible as this was, medical practise of the time forced Maureen to endure an even worse trauma - she had to carry the baby inside for some weeks until the due date.

"I think that was a turning point in Maureen's life," Greta said. "From then on, I saw an awful difference in her. She was very sad, and she became very restless." The couple would soon start changing back and forth between life in Dublin and London, trying to find a balance between the lack of work in their hometown and the lack of family bonds in London.

In 1957, Barney travelled to London alone to see Luke. Barney was fascinated when he set foot in England for the first time.

"He had gotten the ferry over and the train down from Holyhead," Luke recalled, "and he was amazed. 'I never knew there was so much greenery in England,' he said to me when he got off the train."

During this trip, Luke and Barney also met up with Luke Dowdall.

There was more than one reason for Barney's trip to London. He told his son Luke that he was considering emigrating. It was plain that there was better money to be earned and steadier employment to be found in England. Barney might become one of the many men who lived in London to earn money for their wives and children back in Ireland. Luke convinced him not to make the move.

"You tell me what boat you're getting over," Luke told Barney, "and I'll make sure to get on the same one back."

But the problem of finding regular, secure, and decent employment in Ireland was a challenge for all.

"Out of fifty guys on Leighlin Road," Willie recalled, "there might have been only two or three working. Even at that, it was only subsistence work. I remember we'd go to a work exchange to see if we could pick up work even for a day or two - maybe loading up trucks or something like that.

"Even as a boy I remember teenagers saying 'I've saved up enough money to go over to London'. They'd go on the ferry from Dun Laoghaire and then the train to Euston in London. It was what nearly everyone did - to find work."

Maybe those frustrations drove Willie on his course into the tough side of life. He became the member of the family who personified the teenage rebellion of the Fifties. He was the Duffy's 'teddy boy'. "I didn't get in trouble every day," he said. "But most days...

"I used to hang around with the tough guys of the area. I was just a little guy, but even so I used to wind up in maybe three or four fights a week. We would go to dances, and the different gangs would take each other on. You just had to look the wrong way and you were in a fight. How I didn't get my head beaten in I do not know." One of Willie's pals was the neighbour Billy Butler - the Butler family was as big as the Duffy family.

"We used to go to different dances all over Dublin," Willie said. "We'd walk there and back - it could take an hour there and an hour back. Of course, the walk back was where the trouble happened."

Willie used to dance at the social club of Mount Argus - 'the Argo,' as it was known.

"The girls were mad about Willie," Greta said. "He always had style. And Brylcreem in his hair."

He also would wear what were called 'drainpipe' trousers and had lime green socks with 'Rock'n'Roll' written along them. Molly, on a trip to Breda in London, had bought the socks for him.

"No matter how tight the drainpipe trousers were," Brigid recalled, "they were never tight enough. Mammy used to give them to Mrs Hennessy to take them in more for him."

Although Molly supported Willie's fashion statements, Barney was not a fan of his son's appearance. Willie would be leaving the house with his shirt collar turned up - which was the style - and Barney would tell him to turn his collar down. Willie would do so - and as soon as he was out the door would turn the collar back up again.

Paddy also went to 'the Argo' - but on different nights. Paddy loved traditional Irish dancing and would go to the Ceili nights.

"Paddy was a square," Willie said. "He was so honourable - maybe a bit naive. We might go to the same dances, but not together. We'd tend to hang out with different guys."

A favourite dance of Paddy's was 'the Bluebell Polka'. He would push the table and chairs out of the way in the front room to practice.

"He was a fantastic Ceili dancer," Brigid recalled. He would always be trying to get Brigid to go along with him, but she didn't share his enthusiasm for Irish dancing.

Marty Robbins had a big hit with the song 'A white sportscoat and a pink carnation' and this set a trend that was followed by Peter. He would dress up this way going to dances and would also go ballroom dancing. Women were attracted to his dark hair, pale blue eyes and brooding personality.

Greta recalled a time when Willie was pushing his luck at home again. He had been out late a few nights in a row and Barney warned him this night to be home by eleven - or else. Greta could see there was trouble brewing and decided to stay up with her Dad.

"It got past eleven and there was no sign of Willie," she said. "half eleven, twelve o'clock and there was still no sign. But by then Daddy was fast asleep on the chair.

About quarter to one, Willie came in from the dance. I heard him and I met him at the door. He had drink on him - although he was supposed to be too young to drink - and had been smoking. I whispered to him 'your Daddy is inside waiting for you - go to bed', and up he went."

When Greta went back into the living room, she made a noise and Barney woke up.

"What time is it," he asked her.

"About a quarter to one," Greta replied.

"I'll kill this fella when I get him in," Barney said.

"What fella?"

"Willie."

"Sure Willie's in bed ages," Greta said. "You fell asleep."

But it wasn't simply a matter of Willie being off somewhere and not getting home in time.

"The fact is," he said, "if I was told I had to be in by eleven I was never going to be in by eleven. Sometimes it would be raining and I'd be standing out until it got to half past eleven just so I wasn't doing what I was told. I can remember times standing out on the road soaked and freezing - but I wasn't going to go in on time."

Molly usually was the one who kept the children under control, but Willie was an exception to that.

"By the time I got to about fourteen, I was too much for Mam to handle and Dad became the one dealing with me," he recalled. Willie remembered one time when he came in late and was racing to go straight up the stairs to bed.

"I don't know how he did it," Willie recalled, "but Dad got to the hall and even though I reckon I was at least three steps up the stairs, he still managed to give me such a kick in the ass he kicked me up the stairs."

The Scattering Begins

This magical technique of Barney's was experienced by at least one other son.

"One time, I was in a fight out on the road," Bernard recalled, "and my Dad saw it. I came in, knowing I was in trouble."

Barney halted him inside the hall door - at the foot of the infamous stairs.

"Why am I going to hit you," Barney asked him.

"Because I was fighting," Bernard replied.

"No - because I caught you fighting. Now - bed."

Bernard made the fatal mistake of pausing a moment before starting to head up the stairs.

"Suddenly I got a kick up the arse and I was already three steps up," Bernard recalled, laughing. "Then I came down from the room half an hour later and he just smiled at me. Dad didn't hold grudges, and he didn't get angry."

Molly, of course, kept her swing in practice. Ethel recalled one occasion that was a delirious mix of tears and laughter.

"Bernard and Mammy were very close and Bernard would often wind her up," Ethel said. "But sometimes he'd cross the line. One time Bernard, Kevin, me and Martin were on the sofa and something had happened that Bernard had provoked Mammy and she hit him and he rolled over the sofa and landed on his shoulders in the corner. Kevin and I started laughing with fright - so she hit Kevin. I saw this and started to cry. 'You want something to cry about' she yelled at me and hit me. It ended up with me and Kevin crying and Bernard in a heap laughing. But Bernard and Mammy got on really well. She was really proud of all the athletics he did."

Bernard also kept up the family tradition for fighting.

"Someone would come to the door and say 'Mrs Duffy, Bernard is fighting up the road'," Ethel recalled, "and Mammy would run up. If Bernard was winning, she'd stay at the back and say 'they have to learn to look after themselves'. If he was losing she'd push through and shout and stop the fight and give the other boy a clatter."

Tom Carroll was back in Dublin and working at the Guinness brewery, and he and Greta met. They decided to start dating again, and were soon going steady.

Tom was extremely shy, and would leave Greta at the door of 147 but not go into the house. Bernard remembered the time when Tom finally came to the house for Sunday tea.

"There must have been eight or ten of us sitting around the table," Bernard said. "We had been told to behave ourselves, and I remember that Greta was very nervous. Tom was at one end of the table, and all eyes were on him. He took a slice of one of the cakes and put it on his plate. Then, to our amazement, he leaned over and got jam and spread it on his cake. We'd never seen this before. All of us kids just stared at him, astonished. Tom looked up and realised that all eyes were on him. Everything had gone silent at the table. My Dad looked and realised what was happening. The guy was about to disappear through the table."

"Ignore them," Barney said to Tom. "They're all ignorant and they've never seen anyone do that with cake."

Maureen and Austin invited Barney and Molly over for their first holiday together in London.

"I still remember seeing them as they got off the train at Euston Station," Maureen said. "It was a

Saturday evening. And of course Dad being Dad, the next morning he went out for a stroll and found a favourite pub - Lily's on the Strand."

It's worth noting that at this time and on subsequent trips to London, Barney tried to find the whereabouts of his brother Kevin. And at that time Kevin had retired from the army - and was running a pub in London. Barney's sister Maggie, from his father's first marriage, was living in London and was in contact with their brother Kevin. Did the topic never come up between Barney and Maggie about how he might contact his brother Kevin? Did she hide her knowledge of their brother's whereabouts from Barney? Whatever the explanation, the two men remained beyond each other's reach.

Crumlin in London

Ethel, Kevin and Bernard would be up to devilment ranging from roasting potatoes out in the field behind the houses, to smoking - although they would be smoking rolled up newspaper.

"I couldn't wait until I smoked," Kevin said, "because that was the sign of being an adult. The day you could smoke in front of your Dad and the two of you could sit down and have a cigarette - that was the day you were an adult. To be allowed smoke in the house in front of your parents meant you had arrived."

That's the way it was those days. The first time Kevin smoked a real cigarette, however, he did what most people do - he threw up.

"I was out the back smoking," he said, "and I had to throw up. It never dawned on me to go into the toilet, which was an outdoor toilet at the back door, and instead I lifted up the mat at the back door and threw up there."

Ethel had her pals in the neighbourhood - girls like Noleen Hennessy, Rita Murray, Lulu Murray, Mona McCracken - and together they once went on a religious round known as 'the seven chapels'. Along the way, however, they took time out for lollipops and then stopped by the canal at Sally's Bridge to go under the bridge and float the lollipop sticks in the water.

"My lollipop stick went out too far," Ethel recalled, "so I held on to Noleen's leg and reached out - and fell in. A bus halted and a bus conductor had to get in to fish me out - I'd gone down for the third time. I always remember the bus drove me home. There was pandemonium when I got in. Mammy washing me and drying me. I was breaking my heart crying. After I'd been given a drink and was dry and dressed - then Mam beat me for falling in the water."

Paddy joined the Saint Agnes boxing club. Peter said that Paddy's fighting technique was not the greatest.

"If he was going to throw a right punch," Peter remembered, "he would first slam forward on his right foot - and the other fella knew immediately what was coming."

"Paddy wasn't as tough as he thought he was," Willie recalled, "but he'd fight anybody at the drop of a hat. The trouble with Paddy was that he'd fight them fair. Whereas I'd get into a fight and it'd be over really quick because I might give the guy a kick in the balls and head butt. Paddy would put his fists up and be ready to box you and would be dancing around. When I was in fights, by the time you put up your fists the fight's already over. But I saw him take on some pretty big guys - it didn't bother him. He was ready to go."

Paddy had a very distinctive walk that earned him the nickname "here's me head, me arse is coming".

"Paddy had a fantastic disposition always," Kevin said. "He was very kind and considerate, whereas Willie would have been the opposite - a tough nut."

Kevin remembered this time as one when the home was full of activity. "There was the dart board, and the card playing," he said. "We'd even make teams sometimes playing darts. Whoever had Daddy on the team would win. Daddy had won a cup for darts in competition." Another game, rings, was one with small rubber hoops to be thrown at a board with hooks.

"We had great craic in the house," Ethel said. "Mam was always up for fun. Mam and Dad would stay up all night with the boys and their pals playing cards."

"We'd wake up the next morning to the smell of a big fry Mammy had put on," Brigid added.

Brigid's trademark was talking in her sleep. But there was something else for which she was notorious.

Brigid was known for having a strange sense of humour. For instance, Molly had a habit of waking in the middle of the night to go to the toilet. Brigid would also need to go to the toilet, but she would wait until Molly went because she was afraid to go down the stairs in case someone had broken in.

"Usually I'd wait until she'd come back up and then I'd go down," Brigid said, "but this night, I went down while Mammy was still in the toilet."

There had been talk of a Peeping Tom going around, and the toilet was outside the door, facing the back garden. Brigid halted at the wall just at the corner from the scullery to the toilet. Molly, alone, had not bothered to close the toilet door. Brigid leaned around, popping her head into view, and in a deep gravel voice said 'Howaya missus'."

Molly screamed. Barney came running down in a scatter.

"I thought Daddy was going to kill me," Brigid remembered, laughing. She got such a fright she ended up crying. Barney was trying to calm Molly down.

"There's no controlling yiz," Barney said to Brigid. From then on, Molly would check that Brigid was asleep before she would go down to the toilet.

Another time, obviously intent on giving her mother a heart attack, Brigid played a similar stunt. Molly had discovered that there was a mouse getting into the sideboard in the front room and nibbling at papers. She had set a trap in it, and she slowly opened the sideboard drawer to see if the mouse had been caught. In that moment, Brigid had crawled silently along the floor behind Molly and tickled her very lightly on her heel. Molly almost jumped with fright.

Molly wasn't Brigid's only victim.

"She had another evil trick that she played on me over and over," Ethel said, "and I fell for it every time. Brigid might have gone to bed an hour before you and you'd be sure she was asleep. You'd go upstairs and open the door into the dark bedroom. The light switch was just inside the door and you'd put your hand to it and there'd be a hand already over it."

"I don't know how I thought the things up," Brigid said, laughing.

Finally, Barney, Bernard and Kevin planned a revenge on Brigid. They rigged up one of the double beds in the front room so that it looked as if someone was sleeping in it, and rested a man's hat on top of where the head would be. Brigid had been to a Sunday afternoon dance at the Metropole, and Molly - also in on the stunt - Barney and the boys waited gleefully as Brigid came home. As usual, she went upstairs to hang her coat in the wardrobe in the front room.

"I went in and I saw this shape in the bed," Brigid said, "and I just thought to myself 'Dad has brought someone home who is sleeping it off', and just went back down stairs."

Having failed with Brigid, the plotters decided to change target.

"Daddy sent me up to get something from the bedroom," Ethel said. "I walked in and saw this thing in the bed and got the fright of my life. I tried to scream - but nothing was coming out."

Maybe all this was a way for Brigid to burn off some frustration with her place in the family structure. Brigid seemed to wind up with more than her share of cleaning chores around the house.

"Mammy might be going out," Kevin recalled, "and then Brigid would be left to clean up after Luke and Peter. Mammy seemed to expect her to be doing everything."

"The problem for Brigid," Ethel said, "was that the next three in the family up from her and the next two down were all boys - and boys were never expected to do work around the house. So she was always on call from Mammy."

On Sunday mornings, Brigid would be sent to the half past eight Mass so that she would be back in time to cook breakfast for Barney and Peter and then herself while Molly took Ethel and Martin to Mass at nine thirty. Then Brigid would have breakfast made for Molly and the children by the time they got home. She also was working by the age of fourteen - in Cassidy's sewing factory where Breda worked.

Maybe it was because of her work load that Brigid was so skinny. Barney used to caller her 'the handle of a sweeping brush'. Mother Dowdall always called her 'skinny Lizzy'.

Crumlin in London

In London, meanwhile, fortune had smiled on Maureen and Austin again. They won a prize in the Sweepstakes. It wasn't a very large amount of money, but it was enough for them to quit London and try managing a life in Dublin again despite all the work uncertainties. It also gave them the chance to fulfil a great dream. 1958 was the centenary of the apparitions at Lourdes, and the couple went there on a holiday. They were surely hoping to put their sad loss behind them and be blessed with children.

"I'd say the proudest I ever saw Paddy was when he came walking down Leighlin Road in his Navy uniform," Greta recalled. "Paddy could glow."

Paddy had joined the Irish navy, training in Cork. Greta got a letter from him in which he said 'if you write to me, address it to Overseas Duffy' - he was hoping to start travelling the world.

"He was really proud of his uniform," Bernard recalled, "and he looked really smart in it. He wasn't very tall, but in the uniform he looked great. He always wanted to go out in it, and heads would turn."

"Daddy was delighted about Paddy being in the Navy," Kevin said. "It gave the family a bit of prestige - like being a policeman then would be a big thing. And of course Paddy was in the Irish Navy - he was there for his own country."

Paddy was also maintaining his link to his godmother 'Old Mrs Duffy', visiting her whenever he was in Dublin. "He'd come to see me first before going up to his mother," Peg Duffy proudly said. She always kept a photograph of Paddy on her sideboard among her family photos.

"Willie and Paddy were as thick as thieves," Maureen recalled. "Paddy joined the Navy, and Willie also joined up."

What Willie did, however, was not really so clever. Paddy was born January 18th 1940, and Willie on January 21st 1941 - Willie was too young to join. But he altered his birth certificate to read January 21st 1940.

When Willie went to Cork for his training, he was in the same compound as Paddy but not in the same barracks because Paddy had already completed his training.

Willie was six weeks into training before this unusual birth phenomenon of two brothers with an age difference of three days was spotted. A naval officer showed up at the door of 147 Leighlin Road and Maureen happened to be there at the time.

"Is Mister or Mrs Duffy here?" the officer asked.

"Both are here," Maureen replied and brought him in. Molly and Barney sat with him.

"We have two of your sons," the officer explained to Barney and Molly.

"Oh yes," Molly said, "Willie has gone down too."

"Were they twins?" he asked. "It seems odd to have three days between twins."

"Not at all - there's a year and three days between them."

Willie had to leave the Navy and he was back, like everyone else his age, struggling to find bits of work here and there. He then decided to go to the North of Ireland and join the British army.

He was there for about four months when he was arrested for being a member of the IRA and put in prison in the special block for such prisoners. Two things led to this extraordinary turn of events. Willie had been good friends with two other young Irish men in the troop, and it turned out that one of these men was indeed a member of the IRA. Also Willie - having gotten some training in the Navy before being told to leave - was showing more skill than the other recruits with the weaponry.

It was internment without trial, and the British authorities didn't even inform Barney and Molly of what had happened to their son. Molly wrote to the authorities when she could make no contact with Willie, but her letters were ignored. When Barney and Molly eventually found out that their son had been imprisoned, they started a frantic campaign writing to Irish and British politicians for help. There was no response on the British side.

Ultimately, Molly wrote to the Queen of England. It would be unlikely that the letter was ever read by the young woman with the same name as Molly's mother, but someone in the political morass reacted.

Willie was released after more than six months in prison. The Duffy rebel had gotten out of another scrape.

"He was released, given a train ticket back to Dublin, and told never again to set foot in Northern Ireland," Luke said.

Willie was back in Dublin with another temporary job; this time working at the CIE iron foundry in Inchicore. He was hanging out with his pals in the gangs - and he was headed for trouble yet again. Brigid was at home one evening when there was a knock at the halldoor. She opened the door and before her stood a Garda. He wanted to know if William Duffy lived there.

"Mammy was in England at the time with Breda, who was having a baby," Brigid recalled, "and whenever Mammy was away, within a few days Daddy would become ill and take to his bed. The Garda said he had to speak to one of my parents, and Daddy came down. I was sent into the kitchen."

Willie and some of his pals had gone to a dance hall in Ballyfermot. The bouncer, however, wouldn't let them in as there had been previous trouble with one of the group and he had been barred. An argument broke out when the ones who hadn't been barred said that they should be allowed in. The bouncers pulled out golf sticks to attack the group, and in the struggle that followed a glass door to the dance hall was smashed. Willie had told no one at home about the incident. Barney assured the Garda that as soon as Willie came home from work, they would go together down to the police station.

When Willie arrived home, Barney told him "clean yourself up and then you're coming with me".

"What about my dinner?" Willie asked.

"We're going to the police station," Barney said. Then Willie knew what was happening.

Barney promised the Garda that Willie would no longer hang around with the gang, and the Garda agreed to let the matter rest. When they got home, Barney phoned Breda and Gerry to chat with Molly. Then he spoke with Gerry Kinsella and asked him if he could find work for Willie. Gerry said he would bring him into the plumbing trade.

Soon, Barney had organised money for Willie to send him away.

"I was trouble waiting to happen," Willie said. "The best thing for them to do was to send me to England where I could get work."

"Willie had no money when he was going to London," Greta recalled. "I remember Tom and I gave him ten shillings."

Gerry took Willie on as an apprentice. Willie lived with Breda and Gerry for a few months, then found rooms of his own. "Basically, I had left home at the age of sixteen," he said. Going to England was the point at which he quit any further attempt at living in Ireland. The shadow of events in Northern Ireland followed him to London, however. One day, when he was settled in his new flat there, policemen showed up at his door to confirm his identity - and let him know they were keeping track of him.

Bernard, as all the others, finished school at the age of thirteen. A week after, he had his first job. He worked at a company called Industrial Gases. He got the job through the help of Mister Howe whose family lived further down the road. Straight away there, Bernard got involved with the company football team.

"It wasn't that I was good at football," he said. "But I was fast. If they gave me the ball I could run like shit. Though sometimes I'd leave the ball behind."

In keeping with tradition, Bernard was also promoted to the first sitting at mealtime.

"I remember still my first time sitting at the table," he said. "I got a smile or two. I remember Luke giving me a nod. I felt I had arrived."

The Theatre Royal continued to play its role in the love lives of the Duffys. The Royal was having a dinner dance in the Metropole Ballroom, and Luke had gone there with Angela Hughes - who worked in the Royal. Kay Hulsman was also at the ball with a friend of hers who was working for the Theatre Royal. Kay noticed Luke at one of the tables.

"He had a long face on him," Kay recalled, "and I remember thinking 'he's a miserable sod whoever he is'."

"The reason I was miserable," Luke explained, "was that I was due to go in for a hernia operation on the day of the dance. I had gone to the hospital and asked them to change it as I was due to go to this special occasion. They told me to eat very little and to drink no alcohol and to report in first thing the following morning."

When Barney learned that Luke had to have a hernia operation, his response was to look at Luke accusingly and say "have you been with any women?"

While that was the first time Luke and Kay noticed each other, it wasn't until a very long time later that they started up a relationship.

During Luke's recuperation, he and Brigid had a famous run-in. One evening not long after his operation, Luke pushed his luck too far with his sister. Molly and Barney were out and Brigid was the oldest girl at home - therefore, in Luke's male chauvinist eyes, the stand-in for his mother.

"Make the tea," Luke said to Brigid.

"I'll make the tea," Brigid said. But at the time, Luke had left a bottle of cod liver oil on the table and she added, "but you clear that bottle off the table so I can set it."

"Put the bottle up beside my bed," Luke replied.

"Put it upstairs yourself," Brigid said. Luke got up to make Brigid obey him.

"As it happened, I had a few things in my hand," Brigid recalled with a laugh, "one of them being a knife."

Brigid was following a family tradition.

She pushed Luke back in his chair and held the knife up to him.

"Don't ever handle me like that again!"

Kevin recalled this incident differently - saying he remembered that Brigid went the full hog with the family tradition and threw the knife at Luke. Kevin remembered seeing the knife lodge in the door beside Luke's head.

Brigid, talking about the incident with the reasonable-sounding earnestness of someone giving a police statement, said "I didn't throw the knife, I only threatened him with it."

Having fully recovered from his operation, Luke went back to London to find work. In the early Summer of 1958, however, Barney became very seriously ill. He was taken into hospital - he had burst ulcers. The doctors were not sure he would pull through. By this time, Luke was just about to join the British Army - he had passed the medical and they had sent for him.

"Then I got the message about how ill my father was," Luke said, "and I decided to go back to Dublin instead."

Luke was again taking over as the second man of the house. He found work around - as usual, only casual jobs could be found. One job was in the G.A. Brittain's car assembly factory in Portobello.

When Barney was in hospital, a strange request came from one of the doctors to meet some of Barney and Molly's children. The doctor had discovered that because of the couple's blood types, it was surprising they had not produced children with Down's Syndrome or some form of brain damage.

Settling back into Dublin life, Luke went to the Crystal Ballroom on Grafton Street one Saturday night and saw Kay Hulsman again. He asked her up for a dance.

"Are you coming tomorrow night?" he asked her as they danced, and Kay said she was. Kay had gone to the dance with her sister Eva, and when they were leaving the dance Kay noticed they were walking behind Luke.

"That's the fella that asked me if I was coming here again tomorrow night," Kay told Eva.

The following night, Luke asked Kay if she would go out on a date with him - and she said no.

Time passed, and one night Kay had gone, as she often did, up to meet her friend at the Theatre Royal at the end of the show so that the two could have a coffee at Cafolla's Cafe. Kay then went off to get the 81 bus home. Luke, by fateful coincidence, showed up behind her on the queue. He got on the bus and sat behind her.

"I wanted to see where she was going to get off," Luke said, "so that I could get off there too and find out where she lived."

What happened next, however, became more and more puzzling.

"I wanted to follow her," Luke said, "and next thing she goes all the way up to the terminus of the 81 bus where I'm getting off. Then she walked exactly in the direction I would be heading for Leighlin Road. And then she walks down Leighlin Road - and I was thinking 'maybe I'm mixed up here - maybe she's following me'. It was only then that she turned off left toward Fogard Road."

Kay lived on a road that was just across the playing field from 147 Leighlin Road - her house almost directly in view from Luke's. Luke asked her again if she would go out with him and Kay again said no.

Luke then tried a different approach: he turned to God. It was during Lent, and Luke discovered that Kay went to Saint Agnes church every morning for eight o'clock Mass. He then started doing the same - and Kay was seeing him there morning after morning. When he asked again if she would go out to the pictures with him, she finally said she would.

Bernard then became the go-between for the two. He often ferried back and forth across the field from Leighlin Road to Fogard Road with notes.

"Kay would give me a cuddle and say 'give that to Luke', and I'd come back and give Luke a cuddle and then he'd give me a cuddle and say 'send that back' and off I'd go. I thought nothing of it at the time - now and then one of them would give me a penny."

While other brothers were engaged in such things as gambling, romance and rock and roll, Peter had different fascinations.

"Peter had a motorbike," Bernard recalled, "and one day I came home and saw him on the footpath and he had stripped the motorbike down to nuts and bolts. Even the engine was stripped to nuts and bolts. I asked him 'what did you do that for?' and he gave the obvious answer 'because it was there'."

Bernard was always impressed by Peter's intelligence.

Peter's skills and intelligence seemed boundless, but he tended to not follow things through. Kevin can recall that Peter might take something completely apart, and then not have enough interest in it to put it back together. Peter was a brilliant pianist and could play hugely complex classical pieces - yet he couldn't read music and had never had formal lessons. He also played the accordion.

"Our house was never quiet," Bernard recalled, "but listening to someone practicing the accordion is not the most pleasant of sounds. He would suddenly open up the accordion and it was like bagpipes."

Kevin, meanwhile, found religion.

"Kevin and I used to be really close," Bernard said, "but suddenly he would be doing things like going to churches or kneeling praying. He'd always have his hands clasped in the perfect pose."

Kevin took his interest in religion a major step further when he went off to become a Christian Brother.

"I was very religious," Kevin said. "When I was going away to be a Brother, a boy up the road, Eddie Bolger, also decided he wanted to go off and become a Brother. His father said to him 'if you want to be a Christian Brother it's expensive and this and that. But just to make sure you're happy with your decision, I'm giving you a choice. I'm willing to either pay you your college fees, or buy you a brand new bike.' Eddie went for the bike. I didn't get the same offer. I think they wanted me out of the house."

Kevin was twelve and a half years old when he went to the Christian Brothers college in Moate, County Westmeath. This move, sadly, marked the end of the close bond between Bernard and he: it would be many years before they would live under the same roof again.

As 1958 drew to a close, there were a series of highs and lows for the family. Molly's mother, in her seventies, lived alone in the one room flat she had shared with her late husband. Her son Willie still lived across the hall and would care for her. Barney and Molly continued to send the children with deliveries of food and money. In November 1958, however, Mother Dowdall suffered a stroke and became paralysed on her right side. She was admitted to Sir Patrick Dun's Hospital and when she was discharged, she went to live with her daughter Delia who took her in to her new home on Ascal Ribh in Harmonstown on the Northside. Not long after this, Willie Dowdall quit his flat in Pembroke Street and moved to London.

Meanwhile, Barney and Molly's clan was growing. On December 2nd 1958, Maureen gave birth to a healthy baby girl whom she and Austin named Mary.

Barney had recovered and was back home and able to work again. Luke, having remained in 147 to help the family during Barney's illness, explained to Kay that he couldn't find any steady work in Dublin and needed to go back to London. Kay understood the situation only too well - her brother Dessie lived in Luton for the same reasons. She arranged for Luke to stay with her brother and Luke applied for a job at the Vauxhall Motors factory where Dessie worked. Luke left Dublin for Luton where, the following month, he began work at the Vauxhall Motors plant. For the coming months, Luke and Kay could only stay in touch through letters and phone calls.

1958 ended with another marriage in the family. Greta married Tom Carroll on December 31st. Because Tom had a solid job at Guinness Brewery, the couple didn't have to consider emigration. They already had a mortgage on a house in the new Northside suburb of Finglas, and they even became the first couple in the family to have their wedding reception in a hotel.

Barney and Molly

Tom and Greta's Wedding

The End of the Fifties

The Forties had been the phase of Molly's greatest output of children. The Fifties was the decade by which most of them had flown the nest. Circumstances were changing for various relatives of Barney and Molly also. Mother Dowdall had come out of hospital and was living with her daughter Delia, but after a few months this arrangement was proving not to be practical. It was at this point that two old friends of Mother and Father Dowdall, a Miss Mary North of Tritonville Rd., Sandymount and a Mrs Iris D Charles, of Park Avenue, Ballsbridge, stepped in to help. Both ladies had visited Mother and Father Dowdall 'hundreds' of times over the years they lived in Irishtown. The ladies gave their names as references in an application for Mother Dowdall to be accepted into the Royal Hospital for Incurables in the South Dublin suburb of Donnybrook.

Mother Dowdall was admitted into the Hospital on March 24th 1959 and would spend the rest of her life there, being visited a few times a week by Molly, and visited often by Molly's older children. Whenever Maureen and Austin visited, Mother Dowdall would say 'oh here's Doctor Austin' as he seemed to know everything about every ailment.

Molly's uncle, Benny Dowdall, brother of her late father, returned to Ireland to retire in the late Fifties.

"He was bandy from his years on the horse," Austin said. Benny had lived a wonderfully adventurous life, having been a sheriff in Arizona, riding horseback. He must also have had his share of charm. "He told me that it was the women's vote that got him elected as sheriff," Austin recalled, "and also that he was the last horseback sheriff - going out tracking down his man and bringing him back alive. He had a limp because he was once on a hunt after a murderer and was out for three weeks tracking him down and during that time he had a bad fall off his horse."

"Uncle Benny told me his story himself," Peter said. "He went away to America when he was very young. He only had one ambition: he wanted to be a cowboy. He eventually did, and in the end had a ranch with a lot of cattle. In 1951, there were terrible floods and that wiped him out totally. He finally came back to Ireland." This would indicate that he lived in Kansas. In 1951, there was a terrible flood when the Kansas River broke its banks causing vast destruction and loss of farmland and livestock.

Benny had never married. A woman named Josie Boland in Dublin - a neighbour of his parents in Whitehall - was his life-long girlfriend. When he came back to Ireland, he stayed with her.

"We always had a party when Benny Dowdall came to the house," Ethel said, "and we always had to sing. Once you sang, you got a few shillings off him - so you sang like a canary."

"If Mammy's brother Willie also came along," Brigid added, "then that would be a real hoolie."

Willie Dowdall would show up for brief visits in Leighlin Road or to stay with one of the others - such as

The End of the Fifties

Maureen and Austin in London. Willie and Austin became good friends.

"Willie was very down to earth, jovial, very well educated. A chap you could spend the night talking with - and into the early hours of the following morning," Austin said. "You learned a lot from him."

At one stage, Willie was renting a room above Maureen and Austin in a house in Victoria Street. The landlady of this house was a cat fanatic and there were cats everywhere. Neither Austin nor Willie shared her enthusiasm.

"If we saw one at the bottom of the stairs it got a kick up," Austin said, "and if we saw one at the top of the stairs it got a boot down."

This landlady was also puzzled by the fact that Willie spent most of his time with Maureen and Austin, and only used his own room for sleeping.

"Once one or other of us was in, he'd come down," Maureen said. "We'd have a chat or listen to the radio or go for a drink."

On Barney's side of the family things were changing too. The widow 'Old Mrs Duffy' lived in the Lansdowne Road lodge house for 23 years, then had to move out to a flat in Baggot Street, on the top floor over a chemist shop. In her working years, Peg had taken on her late husband's job in the garden. In the end, she had to have a back operation as a result of the years of hard work. Her employers sold the house and it was later run as a nursing home.

Peg Duffy's son Ambrose was about to get married, and he took her on a holiday for a week in London. They would meet up every evening with Patrick Ambrose Duffy's eldest daughter, Maggie, for tea. One day, Maggie arranged for Amby to take a train trip to meet their brother Kevin. Mrs Duffy had maintained contact between the brothers by writing letters on Amby's behalf over the years.

Family traits passed on to Amby. He and his wife became ballroom dancers - just like his brother Paddy and wife.

Back in Leighlin Road, a new romance was blossoming. Peter had met Vera Gibney, a young woman from Drimnagh, at the Olympia Ballroom and they were dating. With the help of Vera's brothers, Peter built an extension to the back of 147 Leighlin Road; the kitchenette. It provided more space for the family, and became the place where family meals were served. The men also built a solid concrete shed in the back garden - facing the door of the kitchenette - for the bikes and for storage and for coal and turf.

The kitchenette extended the area that Molly would want to keep spotless and shining.

"To polish the floors," Brigid said, "we used to be told to slide around them." Kevin was particularly good at doing this. Ethel recalled another time when Molly got a new liquid polish and gave her the job of getting an extra shine on the floor.

"Mammy was walking out from the scullery to the toilet," Ethel recalled, "and when she got to the lino at the door to the toilet, suddenly her feet started racing on the spot and she grabbed onto the door handle. She couldn't stop! All I could do was say 'well you told me to polish it'."

The kitchenette soon also proved useful in another way. Barney still had a couple of his own teeth - at the front on his lower jaw. They gave him a lot of pain, but he would never go to a dentist. Molly was a friend of someone who knew a dentist and made a very clever arrangement. Barney would always come home from work and his few drinks on Saturday afternoon, have his dinner and then fall into a sound sleep. The dentist arrived at the house and all the children were sent out to the kitchenette as the man set about the task of removing the unconscious Barney's last teeth. Soon Barney could join Molly as someone with upper and lower dentures floating in a glass of water beside the bed each night.

Molly's financial juggling made Friday evenings a busy ritual. Sometimes, Martin would be sent down to Floods pub on Sundrive Road to collect the pay packet from Barney who would be having a few drinks there after work. This money was used to serve the procession of men coming to collect payments on various loans or credits; the milk man, the bread man, the pot man, the cheque man, the insurance man - even one simply and bluntly known as the Jew man. Bernard recalls Jim O'Keeffe coming around. This fat red-faced man with bunny rabbit front teeth, who once served as Dublin's Lord Mayor, owned the local grocery store. Bernard recalled that he came around twice a week - once delivering groceries, and then on Fridays to be paid. He drove a Ford Zephyr.

"There was something creepy about him," Bernard said. "I remember Dad didn't like him either."

There was also a saving system known as the 'didley', whereby people paid a weekly sum into a fund for special times of the year - such as the Christmas didley - or for special events.

Barney and Molly

"I've always believed that Mam could have been a great businesswoman," Ethel said. "She had a way of working money and she had great determination."

"She kept a huge family fed at times when other families were going hungry," Brigid said.

In the area, another family had set up a shop as a way to help them make ends meet. The Mahers, in a corner house almost facing 147 across the field, had opened a shop with some groceries and other provisions in a shed at the side entrance of their home. "Everyone smoked back then," Bernard said. "A regular way for me, as a kid, to pick up a few pence was to go get cigarettes for Peter or Luke."

Whatever about how Molly managed the stresses and strains of having and raising so many children, Mrs Maher was an example of the dangers Molly had faced. Mrs Maher, always a gaunt, harassed woman surrounded by an endless flow of children, gave birth to her last child and in the process suffered a stroke. She could no longer speak, and had little use of one side of her body - yet she carried on serving in the shop and trying to cope with her gang of children.

Puberty was unkind to Bernard. He had a severe problem with acne. He also washed his hair every day and Molly would warn him that if he kept on washing his hair it would fall out. Decades later, she was proven right. Bernard started growing his hair long and Molly would beg him to get it cut. He may have been growing it to hide spots on his forehead. The only one he trusted to cut his hair was Brigid.

"You cut my hair," he'd say to her, "but I'm watching you. Just cut that much."

The End of the Fifties

Brigid said he would be watching in the mirror and that she would have to hold up each piece to show him what she was cutting and what she had cut.

"I remember Bernard washing his hair twice a day and spending two to three hours a day in front of the mirror," Kevin said. "He loved himself to the extreme. He had great confidence."

"Bernard had one of these brushes with a strap at the back that you slipped your hand into," Greta recalled, "and I remember he'd take his hand out of his pocket - and the brush would already be strapped to his hand."

Bernard was another Duffy that all the girls fell for. He was always very particular about how he dressed and how he looked, and of course he was a tall teenager with an athletic form: he was the bee's knees.

"Creasing your trousers was the big thing," Bernard recalled. "You'd use an iron straight onto the trousers rather than having a cloth over it, and what happened was that after a while you'd see teddy boys in suits that had shiny trousers as compared to the jacket."

Bernard had also grown very tall - the first six-footer in the family. Maybe it was due to the changing standards of nutrition, but Kevin and Martin would also reach that height. Bernard, however, was the first to change the dynamic with 'big' brother Luke who was several inches shorter. If Luke was around and tried to wield his authority, Bernard would pat him on the head and say 'it's alright, Luke'.

Bernard was, like almost every other working class Irish male in those days, struggling to find work while earning very little. He wanted to find something more secure: he wanted to learn a trade. Bernard asked Gerry Kinsella to take him on as an apprentice, and Gerry agreed. Bernard was going to be yet another Duffy leaving Ireland to find work - though he was only fifteen years old.

"I suppose I've always been belligerent," Bernard said. "I was absolutely terrified, but I wanted to do it and even though Mam tried to talk me out of it she couldn't. It was one time when I remember Mam crying. She took me to the station to get the train to the ferry, and she was crying. You don't understand when you're fifteen. When I think about it, it's scary. She looked at me - and I think in that moment she and I both knew I was too young. I hadn't got a clue what I was doing. I hadn't even a clue where London was - and that's where I was going. I had a small suitcase and a scrap of paper and I was off. You grow up quick."

Gerry took Bernard under his wing - just as he had done before with Willie. Gerry had been a plumber and had studied up to becoming a heating engineer.

"One building we worked in was what is now the Labour headquarters in Millbank Tower," Bernard recalled, "and Gerry was there with a team of plumbers and welders working to him."

Willie had taken to the work and greatly enjoyed it. He began studying to learn more about the craft. But Bernard soon realised the line of work was not for him.

"Gerry took great care of us," Bernard said. "I remember one time, a manager came on the site and told me to clear some rubbish. I told him it wasn't my job. He said 'do it or you're fired'. Gerry walked over and said to him 'that's not his job', and this man said 'well he's fired'. Gerry said 'okay, I'm fired too'. He walked off the site with me."

Gerry Kinsella had a motorbike with a side car, and Austin had a Ford Austin that was his pride and joy.

The End of the Fifties

Even so, the distance between the three Duffy outposts - Breda in Croydon, Luke in Luton and Maureen in North London - meant the family didn't see each other very often.

While Bernard had left, another son made an unexpected return. Things had not gone as planned in Kevin's calling to the religious life.

"It was quite a strict regime," he said. "I was also unusual in that I went to this Christian Brother school, but never had a Brother teaching me. They were always lay teachers. We had a Master Charlie who was strict and used his cane a lot."

Master Charlie had some extra techniques for making the cane strikes hurt, but for the boys it became a matter of pride not to cry. The teacher would swing the cane up and down several times to build up momentum before he would hit the boys.

"It was only on the hands," Kevin recalled. "We'd wet our hands or rub them to try and get them ready. You had to be very careful that he didn't catch you on the tips of your fingers - that was the worst part. So pulling worked against you. The palm was the best. I never would cry."

After his first year, however, Kevin was told to leave: his dry sense of humour got the better of him.

"A brother used to stare at me," Kevin said. "We'd be sitting down at the dining table, and this Brother Woods would be staring at me with a complete dead expression. I decided 'feck that' and I stared back at him the same way. I was told I had the wrong attitude. I told them I couldn't eat my food with him staring at me."

When Kevin returned to 147, he immediately went to work - first as a butcher boy making deliveries, then working in the 'New Electric' cinema on Talbot Street selling ice cream. Later, he worked in a shoe repair shop in Aungier Street. He then started work in the shoe store Fennessy's - where his talents for selling and for being industrious soon made him the protégé of the owner.

The road to the altar wasn't entirely smooth for Luke and Kay. Luke was back in Dublin on a visit and Angela Hughes found out. She came up to 147 on the pretext of wanting to visit Barney and Molly, but at the end of the evening Luke walked her to the bus stop and she told him she wanted to get back with him again. When Luke got home, Brigid knew what was happening and gave out to him for even considering going back to Angela Hughes. Luke went over to Kay to tell her what had happened, and it was then that they decided to stay together and get married.

In July, the big step was taken by Luke and Kay.

"I got home from London on my Dad's birthday, July 19th," Luke recalled. "I met Kay, and we went off and got our engagement ring. Then we met up with my Dad and told him we were engaged."

Although Luke was away, Kay was being brought into the fold of the Duffy family. She recalled one time when Paddy, on leave from Cork, showed up at her door with his bike and invited her to go out for a cycle with him. They cycled out to Dun Laoghaire for the day.

As the new school year began, Martin shifted from his first few years going to the Holy Faith Convent on the Coombe to starting in the Saint Coilm Christian Brothers school on Armagh Road. Unlike his brothers

The End of the Fifties

before him, he had no brothers to back him up. On his first day in school, however, Martin got into a fight. That evening, he told his father.

"What did the boy do," Barney asked him.

"He called me 'Duffy'," Martin replied. Barney burst out laughing.

"That's all?"

"Yeah - he didn't call me 'Martin', just 'Duffy'."

"Lots of the men I work with would call me 'Duffy'," Barney said. "There's nothing wrong with someone just calling you that."

Martin was also making his own contribution to the rich variety of personalities in 147. His particular addition was an invisible friend. It's not unusual for a child to have an invisible friend, but Martin had taken it a step further by saying that his friend should have a place at the table. Given the crush of kids at feeding time, this should have been considered out of the question. But Molly always had a lot more tolerance for Martin, and she would set a place for his invisible friend. This probably didn't add to Martin's popularity among his brothers and sisters. But it made his invisible friend very happy.

"Martin was always odd," Kevin said. Adding to Martin's reputation as an 'odd' child was that he would talk to himself. Brigid remembered times when she would come home from work and find Martin sitting on the railings of the front garden chatting away with himself. She would go in and tell Molly to bring Martin in because he was 'making a show of us', but Molly would say "leave him alone."

Molly also didn't like Martin to play out on the road with the other boys, which is maybe why he invented imaginary company. If Martin was going out to play, Molly would say "go if you want, but I'll kick ya for falling." He would also sneak a football out to play by stuffing it up his jumper.

"You're not taking a football with you, are ye?" Molly would say to him.

"No I'm not," he'd reply - with the football bulging from the back of his jumper.

"Well that's alright then," Molly would say - ignoring the bulge.

Another oddity Martin was known for was that, regardless of weather, he wouldn't wear a coat. If it was raining, Molly would tell him to put a coat on.

The Sixties

The way of life in Leighlin Road settled into a gentler routine as the Sixties began: the place was no longer overrun by young children, and all but Martin were bringing home a pay packet. Most of Barney and Molly's children had married or emigrated. The money struggle was mainly in the past. There had been many hardships and many times when clothes were handed down. Things had much improved, however, by the time it came to Martin's Communion. He had his own - very smart - Communion suit. The school had set a day when a photographer would come to take individual photographs of all the Communion kids - a day on which, naturally, these kids should show up wearing their Communion clothes. Martin forgot all about this and showed up in his usual outgrown elbowless jacket and frayed jumper. The photographer took his photograph anyway. When Molly found out what had happened she didn't get annoyed - she ordered copies of the photograph.

"Martin seemed to get away with everything," Kevin said. "I think sometimes if he did something wrong, I'd get the clatter because Mammy didn't like to hit him."

The Duffys were one of the first families on the road to get a telephone. In keeping with the general community spirit, Molly and Barney shared the phone with neighbours. Martin recalls the many times he - being the youngest - was sent racing off up and down the road to neighbours to tell them there was a call for them. One family, the Howes, had the distinction of being possibly the only Protestant family in Crumlin. They lived half way down the road and received regular calls from family in England.

Having a phone was very necessary for maintaining contact with the scattered family. Willie complained that he would phone up from London to talk with his parents and Molly would spend all her time talking about Martin; 'Martin's doing this, Martin's doing that...' Willie came to resent the attention the youngest got when all he wanted to do was talk with his parents about them and himself.

Martin, meanwhile, was struggling against the dread fate of being a 'Mammy's boy'. He was the only child Molly really had time for and was growing up when her other children were moving away. In a very male-oriented house, Martin had little connection with his brothers or father and a lot of attention from his mother. One of his reactions was that, when he was out in public with his mother, he would not walk by her side or sit beside her on the bus. If they were in town, he would walk a short distance behind her. If they were on the bus, Molly would sit near the exit and Martin would sit at the front: Molly buying tickets 'for me and for that boy sitting up there'.

Martin remembered one occasion when certainly he got very different treatment than was traditionally handed out before to his brothers and sisters. He was on a lunchbreak from school. To make a sandwich, he had taken a knife out of a drawer and a plate out of the kitchen press. He closed the press with the knife in his hand, however, and the butt of the knife broke the glass of the press. He started crying, knowing that he was going to be in serious trouble. Molly came out and when she saw the state he was in she said it didn't matter that he had broken the glass - it was just an accident.

Another time, Martin was alone during a school lunch break and decided to boil himself two eggs. Having the typical Duffy male ignorance of anything that goes on in a kitchen, he assumed that the softer you wanted an egg to be the longer you had to boil it. By the time Molly got home he had probably been boiling the eggs for half an hour. When Molly found out his theory of boiling eggs to make them soft, she burst out laughing. She took one of the eggs and threw it against the wall and it bounced. She and Martin laughed and then Molly halted.

"Oh, it's a sin to do that with food," she said.

On Wednesdays, Molly would go to bingo - often with Betty. Barney would root in his pocket and count what money he had.

"I have the money for one pint," he'd say, "but a man can't go into a pub and just have one pint." Kevin and Ethel and Brigid would put some of their pennies together to give Barney the price of a second pint.

"Dad didn't drink during the week, but would have his few drinks on Friday night on the way home from work," Ethel recalled. "Then on Saturday on his way home from work in the afternoon he'd have a few drinks. He'd come home, and we'd always have steak and onions and we'd listen to the radio and have great craic at the table talking. Then he'd go to his armchair and fall asleep."

Not that he got much peace. There was a family tradition of thwarting his naps.

"We'd go over to him with a feather and tickle him on the nose," Kevin said, "and he'd wake up for a moment and then nod off again."

"We'd rob his false teeth and put ribbons in his hair and put make-up on him," Ethel added. "He'd wake up around five o'clock and then he'd go for another couple of pints and then he and Mammy would go to the Theatre Royal."

After the show, Molly would stand outside Mooney's Pub across the road from the Royal while Barney ran in and had a pint before they got the bus home.

When Barney and Molly went to the Royal, Ethel and Martin took turns going with them. Indeed, with finances becoming easier Ethel and Martin were enjoying a much more comfortable upbringing than the others had known. They were nicknamed 'the duke and the duchess'.

"Martin and Ethel were spoiled," Brigid said. "Ethel had a twin dolls pram when no one else even knew what a twin dolls pram was."

Things had not become so easy, however, that Molly would allow such frills for herself as heat in the house during the daytime. Martin recalled times in winter coming home from school and he and Molly would sit in the cold waiting until it was near six o'clock and the family would start coming home from work.

The Sixties

"It won't be long," Molly would say to Martin. Only when it was time to get the house warm for the homecoming workers would Molly light the fire.

A job for Martin was to set out his Dad's slippers in front of the fire so they would be warm for him to get into when he got home. If Martin didn't do the job, Barney would tease him by saying "I'll get the boy with red hair to do it for me," and Martin would jump into action.

The only times Barney got too drunk were when he fell into bad company - people like his brother Paddy! Sometimes, Ethel would get annoyed with Paddy for letting Barney get so drunk. But Paddy would come in with Barney and a sing-song would start. No one could complain about song and laughter.

Barney and Molly began to make regular Summer trips to their sons and daughters in London. What they didn't know, however, was that their departure meant one thing; party time for the teenagers left at home.

"Mrs Donoghue next door helped us to hide the stuff," Brigid said.

"I remember times when me and Brigid were waving to Mammy and Daddy as they were walking away down the road," Ethel said, "and meanwhile Kevin was out the back taking the beer in over the wall from Mrs Donoghue."

Molly always knew what they were up to, but pretended not to. Then Mr and Mrs Hennessy told her what was happening and so she had to give out to the kids.

Kevin wasn't finished causing problems through his religious calling. He had joined the Legion of Mary, but was bringing his energy and young way of thinking to a group of older people.

"It was very unusual for someone my age to be in the Legion of Mary," he said. "They would do the prayers for this and prayers for that, and I would say 'why are we spending all this time praying when these people are starving - surely we should be giving them something to eat'. I was told 'that's not the function of the Legion of Mary'. After a couple of months, I was asked to leave."

Kevin had a particular commitment to the welfare of itinerants. "They were total outcasts at that time," he said. "I always enjoyed playing hurling, so we formed an itinerant hurling team. We even created a league. We couldn't find many teams to play with us but we got, for instance, a team of Christian Brothers who played against us. That would be some match. We couldn't put an age restriction on the itinerants or else we couldn't make up a team - so it was anything from fifteen to fifty. I was being helped by Father Fehily - who later became a Monsignor - and by Victor Bewley of Bewley's Cafes. He was the chairman of the itinerants committee. Victor Bewley was a lovely man - an absolute saint. Goodness radiated from that man. He gave of his time and money. The most important thing was his time because he gave us credibility." For years to come, Kevin maintained his link with the itinerants and would go up on Sundays to play hurling with them.

Paddy had signed up for a term in the Irish Navy, but he announced to his parents that he wanted to leave and was going to buy himself out. Barney was annoyed about it - he had taken great pride in having a son in the Irish Navy. The reason for Paddy's decision was love.

The Sixties

Paddy had met a girl in Cork, Marie Horan, and wanted to marry her. But he wasn't earning enough money in the Navy for that to happen. Meeting the love of his life had taken the wind out of Overseas Duffy's sails.

Paddy in the Irish Navy

Paddy, stationed in Cobh in County Cork, had met Marie at dances there.

"We didn't do Irish dancing - we did the modern dancing of the time," Marie said. "He was a lovely dancer - but I was equally as good to keep up with him."

Marie lived in Cork City, and Paddy began going there to see her more often.

"My sisters used to say 'he's a proper gent'," Marie recalled. "He was very caring, and very kind."

When Paddy bought himself out of the Navy, he went home to Crumlin.

"He had to show his father his discharge papers," Marie said. "He had to show that he had a clean bill coming out of the Navy."

Paddy then went to London to find work - again with Gerry Kinsella providing the support by taking him in and giving him employment.

Paddy, Bernard and Willie all ended up living within a small distance of Breda and Gerry so they could see each other. It was the London branch of the Duffy family.

"Everybody sent money home," Willie recalled. "It was a chore trying to write a letter every week - and sometimes you'd send the money even if you didn't write a letter."

Willie met Helen O'Hegarty, an Irish woman working in London as a nurse. They met at a night club and started dating. Helen was from Portadown in Northern Ireland and was working in a hospital in Croydon. She had previously been living in Liverpool, where she had done her training.

Paddy had been working for a year in London when Marie, still living and working in Cork, decided that she would go there too. She stayed at first with Breda and Gerry, but later found a flat of her own. How she found the flat showed that Paddy was being his usual self.

"Paddy was very involved in the Church and did voluntary work for Vincent de Paul," Marie said, "He had mentioned to some of the volunteers he was working with that I was looking for somewhere to live.

The Sixties

There was a lady who was living on her own, and she was glad of the company. So I stayed with her."

Marie got a job in the Philips factory.

For a time, Bernard would go out with Willie and Helen and Paddy and Marie.

"Paddy and Marie were totally besotted by each other," Bernard said. "Every time you walked into a room where they were you had to cough to let them know you were coming. They were always wrapped around each other. They were a lovely couple."

"I really idolised Willie that time in London," Bernard said. "For me he really shone out - he was so active and intelligent. He had real ambition. I remember going to a trade union meeting with him once - there was talk of a strike. There were a few hundred men there, all debating back and forth with no agreement. This was going on for hours. Willie sat quietly through it all and at the end he stood up and made a few points that were completely spot on and that no one else had thought of. Everyone in the room looked at him with a new respect - he held the crowd and his suggestions made sense. He had found a way forward that everyone accepted. When we were leaving the meeting, Gerry Kinsella turned to me and said 'your brother is going to go places'. Paddy was the opposite of Willie - very easygoing and happy to plod along. The brothers were all very different. Luke was very strong and determined."

Bernard had been running with the Croydon Harriers Athletic Club. "I used to love it," he recalled. "In my first year, they wanted me to compete in an inter-club meeting. This meant competing in every event. I could do well in the 100-meter, racing against some of the top athletes, also in the 200 meter, and long jump. Longer races I was not so good - I didn't have the concentration."

Bernard used to train with Noel Radford, who held the British 100-meters record. He also trained with the famous Irish athlete Noel Carroll.

"My biggest thrill was being in White City Stadium in London," Bernard said. "All the big athletic stars were there. I was in an invitational 100-meter race. Because I was so young, I was given a five meter head start. The gun went off, and I was thinking 'I'm going to win'. There was only about two meters to go and I was in the lead and I was saying to myself 'I've done it - I've beaten them'. And then - whoosh - every one of them passed me by. The trainer came up to me and told me I had done brilliant. But I was thinking 'last?'."

Bernard was so good that he had been ear-marked for the 1968 Mexico Olympics. He was a sprinter, and as such still too young - sprinters don't usually develop until their mid-twenties. But his potential could be seen.

Elsewhere in London, as a new year began, there was a new addition to the clan. On January 11th 1961 Kay gave birth to a daughter, whom she and Luke named Cynthia. Meanwhile in Dublin in the same month, Barney got a job closer to home in Booth Poole's near the Parkgate Street entrance to the Phoenix Park. He was again working on a car assembly line. This would be his last job - a stretch of stable work in his final working years.

In March 1961, Willie Dowdall was suddenly back in Dublin again and showed up at Leighlin Road, where he stayed. He had continued to live alone and without regular employment, and was in poor health. He had won some money on 'the pools' - a kind of lottery - and used the windfall to make the trip. He took Betty out on a spending spree, buying for her and her family. He also bought gifts for his son William and visited him living with his mother Maura in Dun Laoghaire.

Willie quickly returned to London. Later came the news that Willie had died alone in his flat on Chichele Road in Willisden on Saint Patrick's Day in 1961. He was thirty seven years old. A friend of his, Alfred Sewell, had called around to the flat knowing that Willie had been ill. He saw that the milk bottles hadn't been taken in and went to Willie's room where he found the man lying dead in bed. The landlady had last seen Willie Dowdall the day before Saint Patrick's Day - when he had asked her for a sprig of shamrock.

"I remember the policeman coming up to tell us," Maureen said. "Willie had been living not far from us and we didn't know. We'd been looking for him and we couldn't find him."

"I was with Maureen and Austin at the time," Bernard recalled, "and I went with Austin to Uncle Willie's flat. It was a very drab, sad place. You could feel the sadness. I remember Austin talking to the landlord - who was more concerned about getting Uncle Willie's belongings out so he could rent the flat to someone else than he was about the death. The landlord was threatening to dispose of Uncle Willie's belongings himself."

Martin remembered being alone at home in the afternoon with his mother when a postal worker cycled up to deliver the telegram with the news of Willie Dowdall's death. Molly read the telegram and collapsed in tears.

"He was a lovely man," Brigid recalled. "He was a real gentleman. We always loved to see him come to the house. Once he was in the house, the lid of the piano would go up and there'd be a sing song. The whole night would turn into a party."

Willie Dowdall had never formed another relationship after his marriage ended. A man of great intelligence and creative talent, he had never found a way to fulfil his gifts. Maura went to London with her young son and they stayed with Maureen and Austin.

"Maureen and Austin were a great help to me at the time that Willie died," Maura said. "I got a lot of support from them."

When Willie died, Molly and his other sisters decided not to tell their mother about it as they felt it would be too much for her.

"Willie never comes up to see me anymore," Mother Dowdall would complain to them, and they would always make some excuse for him.

"I was back in Dublin on a visit after Willie's funeral," Maureen said. "There was an insurance policy for Willie, and it had to be signed by Mother Dowdall. None of the others knew how to get her to sign this without knowing what it was. So I went up to see her. I had been told not to tell her about Willie because she was so low and so weak. When she asked how he was I said he was grand. I got her to sign the form without her understanding what it was."

A few months after Willie Dowdall's death, Maureen and Austin decided they wanted to live in Dublin no matter what the difficulties. They came back, sharing a small home with an elderly woman until finding a small house to rent on the Northside of the inner city on Blessington Street.

Austin had different jobs, including collecting the British newspapers from the ferry on Saturday night to deliver overnight to shops around Dublin for sale on

Sunday morning. He also drove around in a van selling paraffin and fuel, and Martin would accompany him as his helper. He finally got a job with Kirwan's Undertakers of Fairview on Dublin's Northside.

At 4.50pm on Sunday afternoon December 3rd 1961, Mother Dowdall died at the age of 79. She had become extremely frail in her final years and had even shrunk in old age: the hospital records that her coffin was five foot long, 18 inches wide and 16 inches deep.

Molly had remained devoted to her, even though Mother Dowdall had been a difficult and distant person. To the end, mystery hung over Mother Dowdall's money. It was always believed that she had kept money sewn into her clothes as well as hidden in the house in Pembroke Street when she lived there, but none was found after her death. And yet, to her death she was receiving a 'gratuity' awarded to her late husband by the manager of Merchant Warehousing - perhaps evidence that Father Dowdall had indeed saved the life of a boss's child. The sum being paid by the time of Mother Dowdall's death was two pounds a week. Mother Dowdall was buried with her husband in the Kilbarrack cemetery on the North side of Dublin.

1961 had been a year of bereavement for Molly; she had lost her mother and her young brother. Tragically, the worst for her and Barney was yet to come.

The Chain is Broken

On New Year's Eve 1961, Ireland's first television station was launched. Dev, now President of Ireland, gave an inaugural speech. Radio Telefis Eireann, broadcasting in black and white with 405 lines, was another step towards the modernising of the still young and struggling nation. The television aerial on the chimney of 147 Leighlin Road had been duly adjusted, and there was finally a chance of being able to recognise what was on television.

Within months, Barney and Molly - and Dublin - lost a beloved part of life when the Theatre Royal closed down. Television was considered to have been the main culprit in its demise. The beautiful building was ultimately torn down and replaced by an office block.

The highs and lows of romance were in the air in 147. Vera Gibney and Peter became engaged, but their relationship was notoriously uncertain. On the mantelpiece of the never-used fireplace in the front bedroom, Molly had a souvenir from the trip Maureen and Austin had made to Lourdes - a model of a grotto. There was a pull-out section at the bottom of this, and Peter would give the engagement ring to Molly and she would store it in this section of the grotto model. It would be fished out a week or so later. This cycle continued, usually to the accompaniment of Peter playing the Connie Francis song 'Who's Sorry Now' on the piano.

"If Peter had had a break up with his girlfriend," Kevin said, "he'd play on the piano day and night - hours on end." Then again, Kevin said he made great money cycling here and there with messages to girlfriends from Peter and, years before, Luke.

On February 19th 1962, the pendulum stopped swinging when Peter married Vera Gibney. The kids in 147 could sniffle freely again.

Maureen's daughter Catherine was still living with Barney and Molly, and Brigid was getting a lot of the responsibility for taking care of her.

"Catherine used to call me 'Mammy'," Brigid said. "If I wanted to go out, I had to either get her to bed before I went out, or get one of the kids off the road to take her out for a walk."

In the end, it was Brigid's protests that pushed the issue. Molly was deeply sad when Maureen came to take Catherine away.

Even if the number of Barney and Molly's children living at home was dwindling, the house was still regularly the scene of parties: people crowding into the kitchenette and taking their turn to do their 'party piece'. Willie Dowdall's widow Maura recalled that the last time she saw Barney was in 1962 - "and he was still the flirt." She thought he looked younger than Molly, who was four years his junior. The child-rearing had taken its toll on her. Maura was by then preparing to go to the USA and make a new life for herself and her son.

Mrs Peg Duffy was still a regular visitor to Leighlin Road, arriving on her bicycle. Kevin, always the joker, used to tease her about the bike and about her other trademark; the scones she had baked and brought to 147.

"They're for Barney," she'd always say, trying to avoid their being devoured by the kids. Another trademark was to sit watching the news on television and give a running commentary on what was being reported. She had, by then, become a grandmother. Amby, who worked for the Electricity Supply Board and later Guinness Brewery, and his wife Jane had two sons, Terry and Alan. Amby was also an avid supporter of the Boy Scouts, devoting much of his free time to that work.

On August 6th 1962, Paddy and Marie fulfilled the next step in their great love story when they married. Willie was the best man.

Paddy and Marie Wedding

The Chain is Broken

"We went to the Isle of Wight for the honeymoon," Marie recalled. "I'll always remember that when we came back Breda had a meal ready for us - and who was visiting her only Luke. Luke said to me 'well Marie, do you know the difference between butter and margarine now,' and I went red."

Kevin, on one of many business trips for his boss Fennessy, was in London and stayed with Paddy and Marie.

"They were a doting couple," Kevin said. "If they lifted a towel, they lifted it together. They were so close - they were one. They were incredible together. If ever there was a fusion of two people, it was them. I've never seen anything like it before or since."

"Paddy was a real family man," Willie recalled. "He lived for Marie, and vice versa. He was a hard working man - and a gentleman. We lived within walking distance of each other, and Paddy and Marie and Helen and I would see a lot of each other." Paddy and Marie also spent a lot of time with Breda and Gerry, continuing a family tradition of card playing with them in the evenings.

Once, Paddy went to Manchester on a job and when he came back Marie announced that she had found out she was pregnant. The wonderful and loving couple were going to become parents.

In May 1963, Kay gave birth to her and Luke's second child, a son they named Bernard. Luke, working for Vauxhall Motors, got a job at their Ellesmere Port factory near Liverpool and he and Kay moved there. They would make their life there, Luke working on the assembly line - as he had done in Dublin with his father - while he and Kay raised their family.

June 1963 was a heady time for Ireland. At the start of the month, the beloved Pope John 23rd died and the country was in mourning. A few weeks later the dazzling grandson of an Irish emigrant, U.S. President John F Kennedy, visited the land of his roots in the course of a European tour and people thronged to get a glimpse of him. Kennedy, in his address to the Irish government, pointed out that de Valera was technically born in America and that if fate had gone differently perhaps de Valera would have become President of the USA and Kennedy President of Ireland. Within months, de Valera would be attending Kennedy's funeral. Death was also stalking the Duffy family.

In July 1963, Barney turned sixty. As he aged, his health continued to disimprove. Two health problems became a constant for him - bronchitis and emphysema. Over the coming decade, these problems would loom larger and larger. But they didn't dim his easy manner and his charm.

Barney was a great storyteller. Peter remembered that Barney could sit at a bar and those around would be enthralled as he spun a yarn. Then just as he was about to reach the end he'd say 'I have to be off, I'll finish the story tomorrow'.

"Something that could be said in a minute, Dad could stretch out for a half hour," Willie said. "An incident about getting a bike puncture could be spun out with all about the man who walked by and the look on his face as he walked by and the story would grow from there."

"You'd get him started talking about something," Kevin recalled, "and he could go on and on about it."

The Chain is Broken

Molly put it more bluntly. "Once Barney got started talking about anything," she said, "there was no shutting him up."

Barney's sixtieth year, however, was to prove perhaps the saddest and most difficult of his life.

In August 1963 Barney and Molly went on holidays to London, bringing along Martin. Paddy greeted them at the airport and gave Molly the gift of a brooch. Martin remembered a time when Marie and Paddy took him off to a park where model boats were on a lake. He recalled how happy Marie and Paddy were together - always laughing, embracing and kissing. The two were extremely happy and very much in love.

Willie and Helen married on August 5th 1963. Having been born a year and three days later than Paddy, Willie was marrying one day short of a year later than Paddy. Willie and Helen had wanted Bernard to be the best man - the tradition being that the best man or bridesmaid role be given to the next youngest in the family. But Helen said that Bernard should get his hair cut and Bernard - being Bernard - refused to have his hair cut. So Kevin was called in to do the honours.

By this time, Paddy and Marie had moved into a lovely flat at 194, Saint James Road in Croydon, London. They were decorating the flat, and also awaiting the birth of their first child. With Marie heavily pregnant, Paddy was doing all the overtime he could get in preparation for their coming child. Life for this loving couple was opening up as they had long dreamed.

The dream was shattered.

Paddy had a motor scooter. On the warm evening of September 26th, 1963, on his way home from work, he was halted at traffic lights beside a hump-back bridge about to take a right turn down the road to his wife and home. The lights turned green and he drove forward. In that moment, a heavy motorbike came speeding along - breaking the lights - and hit Paddy.

There have been different versions in the family of what happened next, but years later Bernard had the opportunity to do some research and speak with police who dealt with the case. He learned that Paddy was thrown from the motor scooter and fell in such a way that the back of his helmet struck a raised manhole cover near the kerb. The impact was at a weak point in the design of the helmet. The metal of the manhole cover broke through to Paddy's skull.

"Every helmet is designed for impact on the top of the head," Bernard explained, "where you have a pressure gap so that the helmet collapses to protect the head and the brain. It's called 'the compression point'. Paddy fell striking the back of his head against the raised metal drain, and the metal broke through. God works in strange ways. Paddy had fallen in exactly the way, and on exactly the part of the helmet, that would cause a fatal injury."

"It was on a Thursday," Marie recalled. "I had Paddy's dinner ready, waiting for him to come home. I could hear an ambulance going up the road - but I didn't take any notice. After a while, there was a knock at the door. There were two policemen. 'Mrs Duffy,' they said, 'you have to come with us to the hospital. Your husband is after having an accident'."

Marie - her baby due in weeks - said that she couldn't go on her own. She had to argue with the policemen to get them to first bring her to Breda's house for help.

The Chain is Broken

"Breda and Gerry came up to the hospital with me," Marie said. "When I got there, I saw Paddy's helmet. I knew the accident had to be something serious. After a while, the priest came in to me."

The priest warned her that it was indeed serious. Marie was brought to another room and was given forms to sign. Marie was then asked if she had family in London and at the time her father was working there. Gerry went away to collect Mister Horan. Willie, meanwhile, had arrived at the hospital with his wife Helen.

"I remember the doctor coming to me while the others were away," Willie said, "and the doctor said 'he's gone'. I passed out. I was overwhelmed."

"As soon as my father came," Marie said, "they gave me a tablet. Then they told me Paddy was dead."

They asked her if she wanted to see Paddy, and Marie said she did. They took her to a room where his body lay.

"His head was all bandaged," Marie recalled.

Barney and Molly's son Patrick Ambrose Duffy was dead at the age of twenty three.

The terrible news had already reached Crumlin.

"The programme 'Come Dancing' was on the television when the phone rang," Brigid recalled. "By then we'd already had two phone calls for neighbours during the programme - and if a neighbour came in for a call, Mammy would always insist that we leave the livingroom so they could have their privacy. So I dived on the phone when it rang this third time - ready to tell whoever it was that we weren't a public phone box. It was Gerry Kinsella. He asked for Daddy. This was very unusual in itself - it was usually Mam everyone would chat with first. Daddy was white with shock when he hung up the phone. Then he told Mammy. We were all going mad with grief. I remember Mammy banging her head against the coal house door."

"I'd been out late working on a day when I'd gotten a promotion and I came home on a high," Kevin said. "I was always playing jokes and the others were always playing jokes. Someone said 'there's been an accident with Paddy' and I said 'Paddy is one big accident'. 'No - it's serious' they said. And then the call came saying he was dead."

Martin remembered being woken by the sound of Ethel crying that night, and thought it was because she had been forced to take in his bicycle which he hadn't brought out to the back shed. He woke next morning to the sight of his father standing before the dressing table putting on a black tie. When Martin asked what was going on, Barney couldn't give him a straight answer. It became a strange question and answer until Martin figured out that Paddy had died. He was sent off to school - Molly feeling it would be best if he were not around. He was later moved up to stay with the family of Peter's wife Vera in Drimnagh.

Brigid remembered waking to the sound of neighbours going to work. 'How can they all do that?' she lay in bed thinking. Life was going on - but life for the Duffys had fallen to pieces.

As was the tradition, the curtains of the house remained closed and a death card was pinned on the door. Neighbours started coming to offer their sympathy while travel plans were being made for Barney and Molly, with others to follow.

Barney and Molly flew to London that morning. Others made their way over by ferry and train. Maureen

The Chain is Broken

went with several of the sisters - she being the only one of them who knew her way around London.

Luke and Kay drove the two hundred miles down from Ellesmere Port.

"We saw Paddy in the funeral parlour," Luke said. "His head was covered. Marie was totally lost."

"I went to Marie to console her," Bernard recalled, "but there was nothing that I or anyone could do. She was completely gone. Marie was a lovely woman, and this tragedy was terrible. I felt heartbroken for her."

Paddy was buried in London, in Croydon Cemetery, Mitcham Road.

"At the funeral was the only time in my life I saw my father crying," Luke said.

Brigid remembered that Molly was weeping at the graveside and grabbed her.

"Brigid," she cried to her, "the family chain is broken. It'll never be fixed again."

Marie never returned to the flat she had shared with Paddy at 194 St James Road, and instead stayed with Breda and Gerry. She was heavily pregnant - the birth only weeks away. Her mother stayed in London with her, but Molly had to return to Dublin. As the time for the birth approached, however, Molly returned to London to be with Marie. At the time, Breda was coping with all this while she also had her own six month old baby, Paul.

"I'll never, never forget the kindness of Breda and Gerry," Marie said. "I was booked to go into hospital for the birth, but there was no way that Breda would leave me. She said 'you're not going into that hospital, Marie. You'll have all those women up there with their husbands. You'll have the baby at home with us.' So she arranged a midwife for the baby."

Paddy and Marie's child, Lorraine, was born three weeks after Paddy's death on October 15th. Willie stood as her godfather. "It was something we had agreed when Paddy was alive," Willie said. "They were planning everything for their baby. They had everything organised down to the last detail."

Not long after the christening, in November, Marie moved back to live with her mother in Cork. Looking back, it is sad that the decision was not made to bury Paddy's remains in Dublin.

"If he was here I would be able to visit his grave," his godmother Mrs Peg Duffy said.

"At the time Paddy died," Marie said, "I didn't know what was going to happen. I had no thoughts of leaving London. Gerry's brother Frank Kinsella had promised he would always care for the grave." A promise he kept.

The cloud of sadness would hang for a long, long time over the family. Ethel remembered one time when she walked into the scullery and found Barney with his face buried in a towel, sobbing. "When I came in, he pretended he'd been washing his face."

Bernard remembered once talking with his Dad about Paddy and joking about how he had the nickname 'Leather arse'.

"Dad completely choked," Bernard said. "I'd never seen him like that before."

Ethel also had perhaps the most awful and tragic story of Barney from that time.

"I was walking down Kildare Road to the shops one day, and I came upon Daddy and he was just standing there breaking his heart crying," she said. "It was as if it had only hit him."

"All the names I called him," Barney said to her. "All the eejits and all the thicks."

"I think someone had stopped him to say something to him about Paddy," Ethel recalled. "I think it really hit Daddy that he hadn't told Paddy how proud he was of him."

"For years afterwards, if any of us heard Paddy's favourite Ceili dance piece 'the Bluebell Polka'," Brigid said, "it would make us cry. I remember once finding Mammy roaring crying listening to it on the radio."

Two years after Paddy's death, Luke and Kay drove down to London with Barney and Molly to revisit Paddy's grave. They were seeing it for the first time complete with its full white marble covering.

"They were still badly broken up to stand at the grave," Luke recalled. By then, the London base of the family had become a thing of the past - its era gone as lives changed in the wake of the tragedy.

Molly and Marie were determined to maintain the family bond with the Duffys. Molly made sure, for instance, that Lorraine was flower girl at subsequent weddings in the family and Marie made frequent trips to Dublin with her growing daughter.

It took Marie decades to recover from Paddy's death. She would continue to have breakdowns of grief. She also never entered another relationship.

Lorraine grew up to be a beautiful woman - with a fine Cork accent. She eventually married, and at the wedding ceremony her Uncle Willie stood in for her father. As Marie put it, "Willie took Paddy's honour and gave her away." The bond between the two brothers had continued.

"We had always remained in contact with Marie and Lorraine," Willie said. "Helen in particular had always maintained our link to them, and Lorraine wrote to me saying she was getting married and asking if I would give her away - and I said that of course I would."

Marie eventually became a grandmother. Lorraine gave birth to two sons - Aidan and Conor.

"I'm always thankful to God," Marie said, "that I had a baby out of the marriage."

Years later, Kevin and his wife Vera went through the trauma of losing two children - baby daughter Renee, and young son Alan.

"It scars you in a way that words can't describe," Kevin said. "It must have been devastating for them. It's unnatural for a parent to outlive a child. Neither Mam nor Dad talked much about what they went through at that time."

For all the losses that had gone before in their married life, this must have been the hardest blow to Barney and Molly.

When Bernard did his research into his brother's death, he learned that the traffic police had later gone to the manufacturers of the helmet Paddy had been wearing to correct the design fault. In those days, helmets were not built to the safety standards that now exist. Maybe in his death Paddy was doing as he had done in his life; helping others. There may well be people who would have died if not for what was learned from the sacrifice of his life. He would not have wished such a sacrifice, but his soul would have accepted such a destiny. He went straight to the arms of God.

New Life and Love

Two months after Paddy's death, there was another motorbike accident in the family. In November, Bernard was a passenger on a motorbike that a car crashed into. The car slammed into his right leg and very seriously damaged his foot - he lost half a toe and three of the other toes were sewn back on. It was feared that he would always walk with a limp.

"When I was in hospital, I didn't tell anybody in the family," Bernard said. "I had been in hospital for a few weeks and they said I could go home and asked me where I would go to. But I was alone - and the only thing I could think of was 'Mother'."

The hospital brought him to his flat to collect his things, then an ambulance took him to the airport. Aer Lingus gave him two seats on the plane. A car was waiting for him at Dublin Airport to bring him home to Leighlin Road. Having left home at the age of fifteen, Bernard was back four years later an invalid whose young life had been spun into confusion.

It was a low time for the family, and for Bernard it was also a time of realising that any hopes he had as an athlete were crushed: the accident affected his balance, so he could never again reach the level of running he had previously achieved. Strong, athletic and active - all he could now do was hang around at home or out on the road on his crutches.

Bernard knew Carol Burgess - she and her four sisters and one brother lived with their widowed father at the top of Leighlin Road. She was the younger sister of Marcia, whom he had dated for a while long before. Now, the two struck up a friendship that developed into a romance.

Unable to work, Bernard was broke. Carol would take him to the pictures. She became the light in those dark days. On December 3rd, Carol turned seventeen. The following day was Bernard's twentieth birthday.

1963 drew to a close. In keeping with tradition, the women had dressed in black for three months since their brother's death. The men wore black ties and a black diamond patch on the left arm of their coats. As Christmas came, they were able to dress normally again. On New Year's Eve, the brothers and sisters had gone off to various events to ring in the new year. If they thought they were leaving a dark phase for the family behind, it was not to be.

"We came home and found there was blood everywhere and Mam crying hysterically," Ethel recalled. "I always remember there was even blood in the fireplace."

Barney had been violently ill and had been vomiting blood. Molly had phoned for an ambulance and Barney was rushed into Baggot Street Hospital - a stomach ulcer had burst. The times were such that Molly was not allowed to go with him in the ambulance. Ethel and Brigid phoned the hospital to find out how their father was and were told he was in critical condition: this was yet another brush with death for Barney who had suffered all his life with ulcers and needed intensive hospital treatment. He was home again within a month, but it was a frightening end to a terrible year in the couple's life. Barney's health had become an ever greater cause for concern, and in his sixtieth year he was becoming a frail man.

1964 was not starting out with signs of bringing better luck for the family. A next door neighbour, Charlie Donoghue, was getting married and people around were cheering him as he left the house. Molly was rushing down the path throwing confetti - and she tripped.

"I remember knowing she was hurt," Bernard recalled. "She said she was fine, but I could see in her eyes that she was hurt. We wanted to take her to hospital but she said no. Next day, she went to hospital. She had broken her arm in four places."

This was a disaster for the running of the household. Mrs Peg Duffy came up to help care for the family. Molly, in hospital, was presented with two choices; she could have her arm in plaster for three months as the bone reset, or she could have an operation to remove the bone. The latter option would reduce to extent to which she would be able to move her arm, but she would be capable of housework within a matter of weeks. She chose to have the operation.

This was the second time Molly had broken her arm. On another occasion, because of her fanaticism about having the linoleum on the floor shining, she had given it too good a polish and went sliding on it. That incident had already limited her use of her other arm.

From then onwards, Martin had a new job. Since the operations on her arms, Molly couldn't reach behind her back. If she got an itch, it was Martin's job to scratch her back.

Bernard loved pop music and could play a record over and over again. Ethel remembered his playing the Marty Robbins' song 'Devil Woman' one night over and over again, trying to learn the words. She was singing along with him. Finally Brigid came steaming down the stairs and burst in.

"If you don't turn that shagging thing off," she roared at Bernard, "I'll kill ya!"

Bernard was fixated on other songs like 'Wolverton Mountain' and 'Spanish Harlem'. While Ethel and Brigid remembered Bernard having a guitar, Martin recalled often seeing Bernard playing air guitar - with a sweeping brush - in the kitchenette.

"I did have a guitar," Bernard explained, "but I didn't know how to play it. I had three or four lessons - but it hurt my fingers. I thought that after one lesson I'd come away playing like Bert Weedon. When I saw how much work was involved - and all the lessons I'd have to pay for - I wasn't too keen."

The driver who had caused Bernard's accident had no insurance, and so Bernard was obliged to sue the driver of the motorbike. The end result of this was that Bernard received the paltry sum of 350 pounds. Finally able to give something back to Carol, Bernard went off to Belfast with her for the day and they treated themselves to a small spending spree.

"We spent maybe a hundred and fifty pounds," he said. "It felt like a million." Bernard bought gifts for the family - Martin got a very snazzy remote control car.

Bernard brought another gift to Martin - something that had existed between the close-knit older brothers but Martin had lost out on. Leighlin Road was divided in two halves by its intersection with Bangor Road. 147

was on what was referred to as 'Upper Leighlin', with its large green. 'Lower Leighlin' was a narrow, snake-like road that turned into a gauntlet for Martin. On this road there lived some tough characters (neighbours and friends of Phil Lynott, who went on to become a rock star through the group Thin Lizzy). Martin was frequently sent on messages down to O'Keeffe's Grocers or to Floods Pub on Sundrive Road, and had to go there via 'Lower Leighlin'. He usually wound up being one way or another taunted. One evening, he was sent to buy a block of ice cream at O'Keeffe's. On his way back, a group of the boys on Lower Leighlin ganged up on him, took the ice cream, chased after him and beat him up. He recognised some of the boys, and when he got home Bernard resolved to deal with the matter. The following Monday, Martin delayed going to school and stood with Bernard by the front window watching kids pass by on their way to school. He saw a couple of his assailants. Bernard went out and halted the kids and brought them back to Martin. In fine Duffy tradition, Bernard warned them that if they ever bothered Martin again he'd go after them and beat them up. That was the end of Martin's problems on 'Lower Leighlin'.

On the Thursday before Easter 1964, Bernard went to Barney with the news that Carol was pregnant. Bernard recalled that Barney didn't react. A long weekend was about to start, and his conclusion was very level-headed.

"Tell me about it again on Tuesday," Barney said to him. "Your Mam is going to be a bit upset, so we'll wait till the weekend is over before we bring it up."

"Even if Molly was the bully and the boss," Brigid said, "Barney knew how to handle her."

Barney and Molly

While routine family matters were dealt with by Molly, in this situation Barney took over. A time was set for Carol and her father to come to 147 to discuss the situation.

"When he comes," Barney said to Molly, "I'll talk to the man. You'll keep quiet. We want no upset about this."

Mister Burgess and Barney discussed the situation calmly.

"Bernard is a good lad," Barney said to him, "and we're a good family and we'll do the right thing by Carol."

Carol's father was of the view that neither Bernard nor Carol should be forced into doing something they didn't want to do. But Carol and Bernard wanted to marry. Bernard and Carol got married on April 30th, 1964 in Saint Agnes's church. Some people had been concerned by how young the couple were, and had feared that the marriage wouldn't last. But their wedding day was the start of a very special marriage, the two remaining inseparable.

Being in Dublin, however, didn't sit well with Bernard.

"I could work again, but I wasn't happy," Bernard said. "I knew I wanted to be a policeman, but I didn't want to be one in Dublin."

If Bernard was thinking of a move back to London, others in the family were leaving that city.

"People want to be able to live and work in their own home town," Willie said. "Things were getting better in Ireland, so Gerry and Breda came back. In London, Helen and I had made good friends with some people from Toronto, and they had told us all about life there and it sounded good and we decided to go there.

New Life and Love

Helen and I had plans to go on a world tour, first stop was Toronto - and that was it. We stayed."

It had been five years since Willie had lived in Ireland. He and Helen spent some time in Ireland before emigrating. In June 1964, they headed off for their new life. "When Willie and Helen went to Canada," Luke said, "they came to Ellesmere Port and spent a week with us first. I drove them to the boat in Liverpool, and they travelled to Canada."

In these raw times, a new tragedy struck the family - one that hurt Barney very deeply. The Kerry Blue dog Tiny, unlike other dogs in the area, was kept indoors or in the back garden. One evening, however, he got out of the house and strayed up the road. He went into the garden of a neighbour who at the time was doing some digging. A fight started between Tiny and this man's dog. The man took a swipe at Tiny with his spade and hit him on the skull, mortally wounding him. Kids rushed to 147 to say what had happened and Barney ran up. Tiny was bleeding heavily from his head. Barney brought the dog to the Blue Cross van that came regularly to the area providing charity pet care. They patched the dog up, but told Barney that the dog would die.

"Dad sat with him the whole night," Brigid recalled, "and the next day when we woke we were told that Tiny was dead. Dad went out to the back garden on his own to bury Tiny."

"I remember when Tiny died," Kevin said. "Daddy was kneeling down in the garden with him in his arms, crying bitter tears. It devastated him."

Aside from the bond between Barney and Tiny, there were many other ties that must have made the hurt so extreme - it was Paddy's dog, its skull had been fractured just as Paddy's, and this was the breed of dog that Barney's father had kept. He said afterwards he would never have a dog in the house again.

Brigid loved dancing and went to all the Dublin venues - such as the National Ballroom, Clery's Ballroom, and the Metropole Ballroom. A friend and neighbour, Gerry O'Toole, worked in the Metropole Cinema.

"The dance hall was over the cinema," Brigid said, "and Gerry would be able to get a pass for me and let me in to the Sunday afternoon dance. When Gerry was finished work in the evening, I'd go with her to a dance - sometimes back in to the Metropole."

By July 1964, Brigid's social life was very busy. She had been involved with some boyfriends but, with her friend Mary Rice, was going through a phase of saving money by picking up a string of dates. In those days, the tradition was for the man to pay for everything.

"Wages for women was so small," she said, "that if you were trying to save up for a coat or shoes, then you met a guy and he paid for going out and you could save your own money."

Brigid and Mary had been unimpressed by the men they were meeting and had decided to 'stay off the scene' for a while. The day they made that decision, Ethel went out with them to Clery's Ballroom on O'Connell Street. They were having a lot of fun and had been constantly in demand for dances.

"I had been dancing with one fella five or six times," Brigid recalled, "and he invited me to go up for a cup of coffee or a mineral - no alcohol was served. But I didn't want to go. I had made my decision."

It was coming up to the last dance, and this man was walking across the dance floor. It was then that another man raced across the floor and beat him to it.

Brigid had just met her future husband, Val Loy.

"I actually said no to Val," Brigid recalled, "but Ethel pushed me and said that was a terrible thing to do and so I danced with him. I was so annoyed at being pushed into dancing with him that I had even decided not to talk with him. But he was so chatty that I started talking."

Val was talking about Birmingham, which he had just visited for a few days to see his brother PJ who was living there. At the end of the dance, Val asked Brigid if he could see her again. It was Saturday night, and he wanted to meet her the following night.

"No," Brigid told him, "I have other arrangements made."

Val explained that he worked as a bus conductor and was changing to the late shift, so the soonest after that they could meet was the following Saturday.

"No," Brigid replied, "I'm busy then."

"How about the Sunday?" Val persisted.

"Oh alright," Brigid relented - not really intending to show up. Mary Rice, however, had made other arrangements for that Sunday and so Brigid, at a loose end, showed up to meet Val. As it turned out, Val had suspected that Brigid might not show up and already had a Plan B. When Brigid arrived to meet him outside the ESB offices on Fleet Street, Val was there with his brother John. When Brigid showed up, John made his excuses and left.

Brigid and Val were dating a few weeks when Brigid went away on holiday with Mary Rice and another friend, Phylis Doyle, on a 'Rail Rambler' holiday. Val asked her to send him a postcard and wrote his address on a CIE 'Lost and Found' docket. Brigid always kept that docket as a souvenir.

"On the docket it said 'Lost - Val Loy, 70 Amiens Street, Dublin 1'," Brigid recalled with a laugh.

Val, Marie, Lorraine and Brigid

On the fine Sunday morning of October 18th 1964, Carol woke up beside her husband Bernard in their flat on Dublin's Northside and told him that she thought her waters had broken.

"What does that mean?" Bernard asked her.

"I think the baby could be coming," she replied. As Bernard recalled, he then did the natural thing - he panicked. Carol was rushed into hospital and within twenty minutes of arrival had given birth to a baby girl - Annette.

Looking back, Bernard said "we hadn't a clue about being parents - or even being adults. We were still kids in mind and in heart."

By the middle of the 1960s, Barney and Molly were well past the hard financial times. There were still debts, and still a succession of people to be paid on Friday evenings. This was mainly out of Molly's fondness for 'hire purchase' - or 'the never never' as it was known; buying things on instalment plans. Times were good and a life's work of raising their huge family was largely behind them.

The changing world was not something that Molly adapted to very well. On one famous occasion, she was using the phone and was being extremely polite. She became ever more agitated. Finally - to everyone's surprise - she started shouting down the phone.

"I'm asking you a civilised question and all I want is an answer!" she bellowed into the mouthpiece.

"What's wrong, Mam?"

"This ignorant bitch says the number I called has changed but won't answer me when I ask for the new number." Molly was arguing with a recorded message.

Some things, however, didn't change. Rats continued to play a part in the lives of the Duffys. An aunt of the widowed Mister McGurrell now lived with him and his son John next door, and one evening this woman got a splinter in her finger. She had tapped at the front window of 147 to ask if someone would help her remove it. Betty was up visiting at the time and went in to help. She had left the door of 147 open, however, and as she returned, kids rushed up to her.

"Betty," they said to her, "a rat is after running up your stairs."

Dublin Corporation had been working on the drains and had part of the road dug up. Betty came in and told Molly what the kids had said, and Molly sent Martin up the stairs to have a look. Martin - in stocking feet - went up the stairs to see if a rat was really there. And indeed it was. The doors to the bedrooms were closed, and the rat was cornered. Martin came down, green-faced, to report the news.

Molly grabbed a sweeping brush and she and Martin went rat hunting. As Martin came up the stairs the rat jumped down. Martin grabbed the bannister in order to lift his feet - and the rat jumped past him. Molly was swiping at the rat with the sweeping brush. This, however, meant the rat was blocked on both sides. It seemed to Martin that the rat then decided to take on the soft target of the unarmed human in socks. The rat leapt up at Martin's feet. Martin sprung up a few steps - better than if his Dad had given him one of those famous kicks - and the rat jumped at his feet again. Molly, enraged, came thundering up and clobbered the rat with the brush. She hit it again and again, knocking it senseless.

Molly was by now as enraged as Martin was terrified. Brigid and Ethel were standing at the front window, screeching in terror. Then Molly swept the rat out onto the path - just as Val Loy arrived at the door. It was his first time ever to come to 147 and this was his greeting. Val turned heel and ran, then finally collected himself and returned to knock on the door and ask

Brigid what was wrong. He was, of course, welcomed in and so began his introduction to Duffy family life.

Val became a very welcome addition to social life for Martin. Several times, Val would take him out on the back of his motor scooter to go fishing off the end of Dun Laoghaire pier.

In 1965, Martin announced that he wanted to become a priest. In those days, there would be a page full of advertisements in Sunday newspapers from religious orders inviting boys to enter the priesthood. Barney and Molly's first reaction was to try an old trick. They offered to buy Martin a bicycle instead. Martin passed on the offer. Soon, there were priests coming from different orders to talk with Martin and his parents. In the end, Martin said he wanted to become a Holy Ghost Father.

This was a tough challenge for Barney and Molly. Clothes, books, uniforms - a long list of things had to be bought. On the list was a rug. Martin saw this and offered "don't buy a rug for me - I can stand on the bare floor." The rug on the list was for the bed. Barney and Molly would also have to pay college fees, and had to make an agreement with the priest - Father Flood - on how to meet these payments.

There was another problem that Father Flood helped with. All Martin's belongings - from clothes to clothes hangers - needed to have his full initials of first, middle and last name plus a given number. But Martin's full name was Martin Anthony Duffy. Father Flood urged an exception of skipping the middle initial, so Martin's belongings were MD 031 - and he was spared a lot of ribbing from the other kids.

Just before going in to the college, Martin was invited down by Marie to have a holiday in Cork. He turned all plans on their head when he spotted a film projector in a shop window in the town. He spent all his pocket money for the holiday to buy this projector and some cartoon films, then put up a bed sheet on the wall of his bedroom and spent most of his time watching the films and bringing in the local kids to watch the films.

In September, Martin joined the Junior Scholasticate of Blackrock College. Breda and Gerry gave him a prayer book as a gift. Maureen and Austin brought him to the college. They helped him with his cases and a bag of goodies - cakes, biscuits and fruit - packed by Molly. Martin left this bag in his open locker and went off with Maureen and Austin to have a look around the Scholasticate. When he got back to the locker room, the bag of goodies was gone.

By becoming a student in the college, Martin was following in the footsteps of none other than Barney's hero de Valera who had been a pupil there and had always maintained his links to the college. Martin would walk the corridors Dev had walked as a youth, pray in the chapel where he had prayed (and where in later years Dev had once stashed a pistol behind the altar) and sit in the classrooms where Dev had studied.

Even though Barney had spent most of his working life either driving lorries or assembling cars, he never owned anything more powerful than a bicycle.

Kevin got a car, a Skoda, but this was no match for his flair. He traded up many notches to a Ford Corsa Classic which stood proudly out on the road in front of 147.

"It was American design with wing tails and four headlights," Kevin recalled. "I put four more headlights on it. It had leopard-skin seat covers and steering wheel, artificial flowers on the front and back windows, white rim wheels. It had a bar on the front bumper full of badges."

Kevin offered to drive Barney to work every morning and this offer was extended to the next door neighbour, Mister McGurrell - the two old men must have made quite a sight in the car.

It was a fine gesture, but one that became a daily struggle. There was one simple rule in Booth Poole's - three lates in a month meant automatic dismissal. Kevin, however, was incredibly difficult to get out of bed in the mornings whereas Barney was accustomed to waking in time to be dressed and sitting, with his cup of tea, waiting for the Radio Eireann channel to begin its daily broadcast with the 7.30am news. The image of Barney sitting there, with his tea and his Morning Coffee plain biscuits and listening to the channel's pre-transmission signal melody, 'O'Donnell Abu', holds a permanent place in Martin's memory.

"Daddy would be up at six," Kevin said. "He wanted to be in work a half hour before he was due to start, so that he could smoke two cigarettes - he couldn't smoke once he started to work."

Brigid would be leaving for work around the same time as Kevin and Barney and she would put on her coat and scarf and go up to the bedroom and say 'come on Kevin, I'm going to work now - you're late'. Kevin would scatter out of bed and dress and rush down - to find Brigid and Barney drinking tea.

"I might do that once or twice a week," Brigid said with a laugh, "but it tricked Kevin every time."

If it was difficult to get Kevin out of bed in the mornings, it was for very good reasons. He had thrown himself completely into his work for the owner of the

Fennessy shoe stores and had become general manager of the chain of shops. At the same time, his entrepreneurial spirit - and perhaps a wish to be as big a hit with the girls as his brothers Willie and Bernard - led him to form a showband. While in the UK and the USA rock and roll had developed a new generation with the Beatles and the Rolling Stones, Irish audiences still preferred the big band sound. Kevin formed and managed a group called the Hustlers.

"I recorded tapes of them and would go around getting gigs for them," Kevin said. "We weren't getting anywhere, and I realised the band needed to be launched. I hired out the Macushla Ballroom on Amiens Street and put the band on. I think six people turned up to see them. And even they were mainly family." As manager, Kevin was responsible for the quality of the act and for getting gigs and publicity - he also wound up doing most of the driving of the band to their gigs.

The band had their set of numbers "you did a fast set, and then a slow set. You played requests for the people, and then you'd have a 'Ladies' request' where the women got up to ask the men for a dance. That's when all the fellas vanished.

"I wanted to be famous," Kevin joked, "and soon found it was a guaranteed way to lose money. We were travelling up and down the country on gigs - doing support act for the bigger bands. This was all part time." It would have taken up all Kevin's spare time - but it was typical of his boundless energy that he would throw himself into such an adventure. Getting involved was partly inspired by Kevin's friendship with the neighbour Tommy Conway on Leighlin Road.

"Tommy was my best friend," Kevin said, "and he was the Al Jolson of our time. He had done stints in the Theatre Royal - as part of the live show before the films - and was a regular in Butlin's holiday camp and was often on television. He was quite famous. He eventually emigrated to England."

Fame was eluding the Hustlers. Other showbands already on the scene and a bit more established - like the Miami or the Royal - started to form an elite of the bands people wanted to see. The Hustlers could not get themselves sufficiently established to attract big audiences of their own.

"We were fighting a losing battle," Kevin recalled, "the band were a dedicated bunch of lads, and we felt we had a sound."

After two years of this great investment of his energy and time in managing the band, Kevin got something of a shock: the members of the band he had formed decided to fire him.

The showband carried on for some years, and some of the band members went on to make careers as musicians. "It was a real rock band and we were great, and given the band's lack of success I probably would have fired myself as their manager," Kevin said. He made no more forays into the entertainment business, although his entrepreneurial spirit continued to blossom. It was a spirit Barney and Molly always encouraged in their children.

"We all wanted to get out and do things," Kevin said. "Mam and Dad never said 'you're mad' or 'you're stupid' - they quietly encouraged you, and they enjoyed the variety and the diversity of us all and what we were up to. They could have been a negative force, but they wanted to see us get out of the rut."

Barney and Molly

Father of the Brides

Brigid and Val announced that they would get married in September 1966. They soon found an ideal flat on the North side of the city, however, and were keen to rent it. But they couldn't afford to pay all those months while waiting for the wedding. They decided to bring the marriage forward to February - giving six weeks' notice to Barney and Molly of their intention to marry.

"For weeks, Mammy wouldn't talk with me," Brigid recalled. "She was convinced I was pregnant."

A few weeks before Brigid and Val's wedding, Ethel went to the Arcadia in Bray to see the spectacular double bill of Tom Jones and Dickie Rock in concert. At this event she met the tall, handsome, athletic Derek Carruthers. It turned out to be a meeting that suited each of their short term needs.

"In those days, you didn't pay when you went out with a fella so I was looking for a boyfriend so I could save for the summer," Ethel said, "and Derek was in a cycle club that had an annual dance and he was looking for a girlfriend to bring to that."

Their story lasted somewhat longer.

Derek was from Terenure and coincidentally Barney knew of his father: who was a trade union representative in Guinness, and even his grandfather:

who had been a policeman in Dublin. Molly and Barney both took a shine to Derek. Derek and Barney would sometimes go for a pint together. Derek was another man from a small family - like Austin - who was attracted to the rich family life of the Duffy clan. In this short space of time, one unmarried daughter was headed for the altar and the other had met her future husband.

As Brigid's wedding day was approaching, however, Molly was taken in to hospital to have gall stones removed. Aside from anything else, this added to Brigid's work load at home - in between her own preparations, she was also redecorating the house and her own new home.

Molly had only been out of hospital a few days before the wedding day, and on the morning of her wedding Brigid was on her knees cleaning out the fire grate so that the fire would be ready to light that evening when her parents got home. Barney walked into the room and saw her.

"Brigid will you get up," he said to her. "You're like Cinderella."

Brigid and Val were married in the newly built Saint Bernadette's Church on Sundrive Road on the 19th of February 1966. They went on honeymoon to a family friend of Val's in Wigan, England, and also visited Luke.

A few weeks after this marriage, Molly was back in hospital - she had been rushed into the Coombe Hospital. Her womb was removed. Brigid recalled arriving to visit Molly in the ward just as Barney was leaving. He looked deeply upset.

"Don't go in, Brigid," he said to her, "she's just come out from under the anaesthetic."

Brigid wanted to go in and so Barney went with her, not wanting her to be alone.

When Brigid saw Molly she was shocked and burst into tears.

"I thought she was dying," Brigid recalled. Molly recovered, but both she and Barney were showing the physical strains from the years of poverty and hardship they had endured. It was a cruel irony: as times were getting easier, the couple were becoming more prone to illness.

Ethel and Derek

On March 8th 1966, something happened that would surely have brought a smile to Barney. It was the fiftieth anniversary of the Easter Rising - in which he had taken part. Someone decided a rather special way of marking the event: in the middle of the night, they blew up Nelson's Pillar. The explosion blew away Admiral Nelson, who had been lording over Dublin's main street for almost a hundred and fifty years. More than half the pillar remained, however, and when the Irish Army set another explosion to remove this stump, they caused more damage to surrounding buildings on O'Connell Street than had been caused by the initial explosion.

By the summer of 1966, Martin could bring a somewhat unusual bit of cultural cross-fertilisation to Crumlin. Blackrock College was famous for its rugby teams and Martin, like all students there, played rugby at least twice a week. He had come to enjoy the game, and had his own rugby ball which he brought home on the summer holiday. Rounding up friends from around the roads, Martin organised training sessions in rugby on the field in front of 147 and was refereeing games of rugby being played by boys who up to then had only ever played Gaelic football or hurling. Maybe Barney and Molly looked out from 147's front window in puzzlement at this. Martin was sticking to his reputation of being odd.

There was a Christmas family routine that Martin vividly remembered, as he would be allowed to tag along for the ride. While Molly prepared the Christmas dinner, Kevin would take Barney in his car for a lap of honour around the sons and daughters and their families. Every year, Molly made the same request to everyone - 'don't give your Daddy anything to drink.' Every year, each son and daughter visited would say to Barney 'you'll have just the one'. And every year, Kevin and Martin would arrive back home with Barney drunk and struggling to stay awake and eat the big dinner set before him on the table.

Later on Christmas Day the sons and daughters - having eaten their own dinner with their children - would descend on 147 for evening tea as Barney resurfaced from his after-dinner sleep.

The lead up to Christmas had, by then, reached industrial proportions in Molly's kitchen as she made her delicious Christmas puddings for her own home and also for her sons and daughters. The ingredients would be piled into an enormous basin and stirred for hours - Martin being drafted in to help with the work - and finally perhaps a dozen puddings in ceramic bowls would take their turns on the oven being boiled for hours upon end so that the kitchenette was transformed into a steam room. Molly made so many puddings that she usually still had at least one stuck up at the back of the wardrobe in the front bedroom for Easter.

Bill and Helen visit 147

Willie and Helen made a holiday trip home for the Christmas of 1966. Martin recalled that Willie then smoked rum-flavoured cigars. The couple were dazzling: they were prospering in Toronto, living in an apartment and both working. They were already sounding American. They headed back home at the start of January 1967. A week later, Molly had fallen ill and was taken into hospital. She needed an operation and stayed in hospital for a month.

Bernard and Carol had moved back to Crumlin. They lived just a few doors down from Barney and Molly, sharing a house with the widower Mister Tierney. Bernard worked on an assembly line for Pedigree Prams. Aside from being a fit young man, he was also a diligent worker. It turned out that he was too diligent.

"The money was awful. But the more you produced, the more money you got," he said. "You worked in a team of four or five people, and I like to be busy rather than sit around. But there was a rule setting the maximum number of prams that could be done by a team in a day. Things that other people would wait around for the machine to do, I would do myself. The guys I was working with started complaining that I was working too quick."

A shop floor union rep went to Bernard and told him he was working too fast and to slow down. Bernard refused, and the rep went away. He came back again, however, and told Bernard that if he didn't slow down, the other workers would make life hell for him. Bernard socked the man in the jaw - and ended up losing his job.

He dreaded telling Barney, who was such a strong union man. But when Barney heard what happened he supported his son, saying Bernard had stood up for his principles.

By then, however, Bernard was waiting to be taken into the London Metropolitan Police, having applied for the job in 1965 and passed all exams. Bernard had already gotten A-Levels in subjects such as Mathematics and English, but as part of the application process he had to do a written exam on English history.

"I wrote the exam as a letter," Bernard recalled, "and said 'dear sir, I am from Ireland. I am aware of the fact that you have a Queen and sometimes a King. My favourite British person was and always will be Winston Churchill, apart from that my knowledge of English history is nil.'"

Bernard passed the exam.

There was a delay to his being given a start date, however, because Bernard had been too honest and exact in giving them his work record.

"I listed every job I'd ever had - be it even something for a couple of weeks somewhere, and it took them a year to get references back from all these places."

In late April 1967, Carol was due her second baby and Bernard was away in London where he was going through some last details in the process of joining the police. There was a date set when Carol was due to go into hospital, but on April 23rd she suddenly went into labour at home. Molly and Mrs Sheridan - who lived on the other side of the Tierney house - helped her. The baby came very quickly and was born before an ambulance arrived. Molly had helped bring her granddaughter Karen into the world.

Shortly after this, in June 1967, Bernard started training for his new job in the London Metropolitan Police. It was the realisation of a long-held dream.

At one point during his training, the recruits were at a swimming pool and were lined up around the side.

"Right," the instructor Charlie Fogg said, "everybody up to the top board and jump."

Bernard heard this and thought of a word similar to his instructor's surname: Bernard couldn't swim.

"We had gone into the pool area in alphabetical order," Bernard recalled, "and so I was near the front going in. But the line for the diving board started from the back, so I was one of the last to go up. Some guys were amazing swimmers and could dive off and do loops, most ran up and just jumped. I sped up the ladder and got to the top and I was about to run when I screeched to a halt - I was a long way up! The water looked like a mile away. I heard the instructor."

"Duffy!" Charlie Fogg roared at him.

Bernard closed his eyes, stepped forward, and walked off the diving board. He plunged into the water.

"I remember sitting there, at the bottom of the pool, bubbles coming out of my mouth, and I was calmly saying to myself 'Bernard - you're drowning'," he recalled. "Then I became aware that from both sides of the pool there were splashes - people were diving in. They carried me to the surface and dragged me out of the pool."

"What happened?" the instructor asked him.

"I can't swim, sir," Bernard replied.

"Why didn't you tell me you couldn't swim!"

"You never asked me."

Charlie Fogg later put Bernard on the rugby water team as a way of getting him comfortable in water. But

Bernard's sense of discipline and obedience won him the appreciation of the instructor.

"A big thrill for me was that one day my Dad turned up at the training school at Hendon," Bernard recalled. "I was in a PT lesson, and I was told I had a visitor. In fact, you weren't allowed to have visitors. I went out - and my Dad and Luke were there. Dad wanted to see me and what I was doing."

Barney and Molly had regular holidays with Luke and Kay. One time, Luke and Kay and their first two children, Bernard and Cynthia, went with Barney and Molly on a holiday driving through Scotland.

"We drove up, and on the first night we stayed in a place in the border town of Moffat," Luke said, "and then we were going further up into the highlands. We had looked around Loch Loman and it was getting later in the afternoon and we decided we should find somewhere for the night. Everywhere we tried was packed out. It was getting later in the evening, and it got to the stage, up in these mountain roads, that we couldn't see in front of us. We took a vote and decided that the safest thing was to pull in and have a sleep in the car where we were."

Kay said she remembered that night all too well. As soon as she'd settled down the children, Molly would let out one of her snores and the child was wide awake again. Eventually, everyone managed to get some rest.

"We woke up in the early morning," Luke said, "thinking we'd get out and stretch our legs before starting off on our way. As soon as we got out, we were invaded by millions of midges. We had to dash back into the car. We drove to Fort William, where we found a place to have breakfast and clean up."

Barney and Molly on Holidays with Luke and Kay

As from the earliest times, there was a specially close bond between Luke and Barney. Even though the two were fathers and had worked together, however, Luke still had difficulty seeing Barney as an equal - and this once led to a comical solution to a little problem.

"My Dad had a habit of smoking no matter where he was," Luke recalled. "In those days that was no problem. But he had the habit of smoking in the bathroom when he was shaving. On a number of occasions, he would stub out the cigarette in the hand basin and just leave it there. Kay was the one who was cleaning around the house, and after a few times she came to me and said I would have to have a word with my Dad to stop him doing this. But I didn't know how to do it - how do you tell your Dad to do something?"

A few days later, Luke was still wondering how to bring the matter up. He saw his opportunity when he came out to the hall downstairs with his two year old son Bernard just as Barney came out of the bathroom above. Luke grabbed little Bernard.

"If I ever see you smoking in the bathroom again and leaving the cigarette in the basin," he said to the child, "I'll bloody strangle you."

Barney nearly fell down the stairs laughing. He'd gotten the message.

Martin's time in Blackrock College lasted two years until, in the end, he decided to leave and was told to leave simultaneously. The biggest reason for his wanting to leave was that all the priests in the college and in the retirement house on the grounds seemed so grim and unhappy. Martin had also lost a mentor. Father Flood had been replaced as head of the Scholasticate by the dour Father Curtin with whom Martin had many a run-in. Martin wrote home announcing his decision to leave, and the following Sunday Kevin arrived at the college to visit him. Kevin gave Martin sweets and money and told him that the family wouldn't mind if he left college.

When Martin made his next Sunday trip home, however, Molly was furious that he was letting the family down. Barney took a softer view.

"Always remember," Barney told Martin, "you don't owe us anything." Barney was also very ill at that time, and told his son that he feared he wouldn't see the Summer.

When Martin left college, his first full-time job was as a dish washer in a café in Marlborough Street. Jeered by his brother Kevin, he quit after one night's work and set his sights higher. Answering an advertisement, he joined a long queue of boys applying for the job of apprentice projectionist at the Kenilworth Cinema in Harold's Cross. He got the job. At the age of fifteen, he became the last member of the Duffy family to bring home a pay packet - ten shillings a week - and hand it to his mother. By then, there was only one sitting for meals.

Molly loved to go playing Bingo - usually at the National Stadium on South Circular Road. Indeed, she had a slight leaning towards gambling - probably developed from her years of juggling money to keep the family going. She would often go into plans about "if I won the Pools I'd..."

One night, Martin was alone at home in bed when Molly returned and called him. He jumped out of bed and ran to the top of the stairs. Molly was just in the door and looked up to him.

"Here," she said to him casually, and flung a wad of notes that scattered on the stairs. She had won the main prize of the evening.

Even though the family was now far flung and there were few still living at 147, Molly kept up a tradition of always remembering her children's birthdays and always doing something to make the day special.

"I was married and still working in Cassidy's," Brigid recalled, "and on my birthday Mammy and Betty came in to me at my lunchbreak with a bunch of flowers and a present."

Brigid and Val's new life together was struck by an early tragedy when Brigid miscarried her first child due to food poisoning.

"After coming out of hospital, I went up to stay at Mam's because Val was going onto the late shift and I didn't want to be alone," Brigid recalled. It was a Saturday night, and Ethel was there too.

"Are you not going out?" Brigid asked Ethel.

"No," Ethel replied. She and Derek were having an argument. Then the phone rang and it was Derek trying to patch things up - but this turned into another argument. Ethel slammed down the phone.

"Then the two of us looked at each other," Brigid said, "and we threw our arms around each other and started roaring crying."

Derek moved to London in October of 1967 to train for the Metropolitan Police - as his future brother-in-law had done - and the romance with Ethel was kept alive by phone calls and letters.

Derek's move to England, however, coincided with an outbreak of the dread Foot and Mouth Disease in that country. Ireland had not suffered the disease - which could cause the wiping out of herds of livestock - since 1941. Barney told Ethel that after she had read Derek's letters she would then have to burn them.

"This went on for the first four or five letters," Ethel recalled, "but I cried so much each time I burned a letter, he gave up."

"I don't give a damn if the whole place is destroyed with Foot and Mouth," Barney finally said to Ethel. "It's not worth looking at you crying."

Ethel could keep the rest of the letters from Derek.

Derek came home at Christmas time and the couple planned on getting engaged.

"It was traditional for the man to ask Daddy's permission to get engaged," Ethel said, "and we had come home late the night that Derek wanted to ask Daddy for my hand. Daddy was asleep, but we were picking up the engagement ring next day so I went up and woke him and said Derek wanted to speak with him."

Barney came down and he and Derek went into the kitchenette while Ethel sat in the living room with Molly. Kevin was also there and he knew what was going on. Derek was friends with some of the members of the Irish ballad group The Wolfe Tones, and they had a song out called 'Treat my daughter kindly'. Kevin kept playing the record over and over again while Derek was trying to have his serious conversation with Barney.

When Ethel was getting ready to get married, she was sewing clothes and Barney sat to chat with her.

"One thing I always admire about your Ma," he said to Ethel, "is that she always dresses well and keeps herself well. And if I ever say to her that she has something on that I don't like, I'll never see it again. She won't say anything at the time, but that would be that."

Barney spoke to Ethel several times as the marriage date was approaching, wanting to be sure that she was happy with what she was doing. Ethel believed it was something he would have talked about with all of his children.

"Are you a hundred percent sure you're happy with this," Barney asked Ethel.

"I am happy," Ethel once said, "but could you imagine turning around to Mammy and saying I was changing my mind."

"Don't worry about your mother," Barney assured her.

Ethel and Derek married on June 1st 1968. It was Barney's last time to walk a daughter up the aisle. Brigid - three months pregnant - was one of the bridesmaids. Derek's sister Frances was the other.

Father of the Brides

Barney's last time as 'Father of the Bride'

Something very unusual happened to Barney and Molly as a consequence of the wedding; they were free to share a bed again.

"I can remember how embarrassed they were," Ethel said. "Mammy was mortified that anyone would know that they were sleeping in the same bed."

"Daddy thought it was funny how embarrassed she was," Brigid added.

"Nobody was supposed to tell anybody they were back sleeping together," Ethel said.

Barney, however, made no hesitation. He was back sharing a bed with Molly from the night of Ethel's wedding. This was also a boon for Martin who, at sixteen, had a bed to himself for the first time in his life.

Ethel and Derek emigrated to London, where Derek continued his training in the London Metropolitan Police. In the following years they would have the first two of their four children. At the christening of their daughter Sandra, Ethel fulfilled a - small - lifelong quest when she noticed the name of the church. It was the church of Saint Ethelburger. Appropriately, the saint had been a princess.

Bernard's career in the police force go off to quite a start. He had been through the two year probationary period and had already been out on a beat on what were called 'puppy walks' - a new recruit going out with an experienced officer.

A few nights before he would make his first 'beat' alone, Bernard was walking home from work when a couple of men somehow recognised him as a policeman. One of these men shouted 'hey copper'. Bernard glanced back as a penny thrown by this man whizzed past his head. Bernard went over to the men and told them off and then carried on home. The main antagonist was a tall and very strong black man named Norman.

Then came Bernard's first night alone on his beat.

"I was walking along, in uniform, and saw Norman and two other men standing outside a coffee stall," Bernard recalled. "As I walked by they started more jeering and so I went back and told them not to be stupid. They kept up their insults and I told them to move on as they were obstructing the footpath. They were still being rude, so I arrested Norman for 'willfully obstructing the highway - Section 1.21 of the Highways Act 1959'. I grabbed him - and then his two mates tried to grab him off me. Suddenly, a big punch-up broke out. Norman head-butted me in my ear and my helmet flew off. I completely lost my cool. I remember hitting him hard with a perfect punch and he flew through the air and hit off a railing and slumped to the ground. I thought 'my God I've killed him - my first night out and I kill someone'. But he got up and started to run away so I went after him and had him on the ground. I had him in a grab and he was mine. His two mates came to try take him away from me. Again, I lost it completely. It was the first and only time I pulled out my truncheon. I said 'first bastard that comes near me, I'll scalp him and he'll be dead'. They came for me and I whacked Norman and he was out cold - he was going nowhere. Then, I could hear in the background the bells of a police van. A bus inspector had seen what was happening and had called the police.

"Next morning, I was in court with Norman and he was sentenced to six months for assaulting a police officer. He later went back to an appeal court to challenge the sentence and the judge did indeed change it - to nine months imprisonment."

As it turned out, Bernard and Norman became friendly in the years to come. Another twist to the tale was that one of Norman's mates was a British Amateur Heavyweight Boxing champion. It had been a formidable line-up of opponents to take on, but Bernard the athlete was fortunate to have enough adrenaline and strength to get him through his first-night challenge.

While Bernard was walking his beat on the streets of London, his brother Kevin had become very security conscious back home in 147. "If I came home at night and the house was empty," he recalled, "I'd stand at the back door and shout back inside 'no hold on to the dog - I'll be back in now', or I'd put on different voices as if there was a gang of people at home. If I heard a noise out the back I'd open the door and bark like a dog."

While Barney had said, after the death of his dog Tiny, that there would never be a dog in the house again, Martin had bought a little mongrel pup whom he named Max. This dog, unfortunately, caught distemper and died - though he lived long enough to pose on Molly's lap for the wonderful photo of her with sunglasses sitting in the back garden of 147.

Presumably with his security worries in mind, in early 1968 Kevin came home one day with a gift for Martin: what seemed like a bundle of white fluff that he held out. It was a Wicklow Collie pup, all white except for a black eye patch and a black patch on his side. Despite Barney's sadness after the loss of Tiny, he took a shine to this dog - named Sam - who in turn, like Tiny, became completely devoted to Barney.

Sam would always sit at Barney's feet. While some complained that Ethel and Martin had been spoiled by Molly, it could also be said that Barney spoiled Sam. When the ice cream van came around, playing the chime, the dog would go over to the window and whine. Then Barney would go out and buy him an ice cream cone.

"Sam wasn't a dog, he was another child," Ethel joked. "He was the replacement for Martin and me."

Martin recalled how interested Barney was in seeing to it that Sam lived a full life as a dog. He once arranged for a friend to take Sam away to be 'blooded' - to have the experience of chasing and killing an animal. Also, Barney found a neighbour with a Wicklow Collie bitch and had them mated so that Sam could be a father. Barney also instructed Martin to go get animal portions such as sheep's head from the butchers shop to feed to Sam.

Father of the Brides

From Grand Canal to Swimming Pool

Life became comfortable for Barney and Molly. By the end of the Sixties, just Kevin and Martin where at home. The house would still burst with life on Sundays when the sons and daughters would come with their spouses and children, but aside from that life in 147 was quiet and easygoing.

Prudishness was still alive and kicking in the family, however. Brigid was pregnant and Ethel would sometimes phone from London enquiring - but the pregnancy was referred to as 'Brigid's sore leg'. On January 24th 1969, Brigid gave birth to her first daughter, named Aisling: the Irish for 'vision'.

Early in 1969, Molly was doing one task she regularly took upon herself - helping a daughter who was giving birth. Ethel and Derek were in Stepney, London, in an apartment block that was a housing estate for the Metropolitan police. Ethel was near the end of her first pregnancy, and Molly travelled over to be there for her. In her stay, Molly wrote some letters. They are beautiful in the way they show how much love she felt for her husband and children and how much she missed her own home.

From Grand Canal to Swimming Pool

Here are quotes from letters she wrote to Barney over a month long absence between February and March 1969. All letters were addressed 'Hello Barney':

I hope everything is alright at home and that you are getting your food. As you can see I arrived safe... Everything is fine over here, but very very cold. I hope Ethel is well soon. She looks great. I was up in Bernard's on Monday. He looks very well, also Carol and children - they got very big and she has a house. Bernard passed his final exam 193 out of 200. He was short 7 for a star.

How is my son Kevin. Tell him I miss him a lot. Also the baby. I hope they are looking after themselves alright and not staying out late.

It is a very lonely place. Good luck and God Bless you all. Keep smiling.

PS; I hope you are getting your hot water bottle.

I hope all is well at home and that some of them are going up to give you a help out. I don't go out much because Ethel can't go out. It is a very lonely place - very quiet. It is near Pettycoat Lane but I can't go, and for the Masses I just can't take to it at all. How is Betty? Is she home from hospital? I hope she is better. I miss my bingo a lot. It's all flats over here, very few shops. Say a prayer Ethel is right soon as I feel very lonely here. Bernard lives a good bit away. There's not a bother on him. The way Bernard looks he would arrest his own mother-father.

Keep smiling. I'm not dead.

Tell some of them to write please.

I am glad Ethel is alright because it is very lonely over here. You wouldn't see anyone to talk to. Everyone keeps to themselves and Ethel won't be home for ten days on March 11th. Ciaran will be christened on March 16th, then I go home.

Ethel would be lost if I didn't go up to her. She would be on her own until Derek goes up at 7-8pm every night.

How are Luke and Kay enjoying their holidays? How is Brigid, Betty and all the gang?

I am writing to let you know I will be home on Sunday night. Tell Martin I got the shamrock thanks. See you on Sunday night.

The letters were always signed 'Your Moll', with kisses for Barney and for the two children at home; Kevin and 'the baby' - eighteen year old Martin.

Through his work in Fennessy's, Kevin had met Vera Malone - a young woman from Cabra. They started dating and soon were going steady. Around the same time, Kevin had decided to go into business on his own, opening Duffy's Shoe Store on Aungier Street. It was a brave step that his old boss had tried to discourage, but Kevin poured his energy into building up his own business and in due course he had a chain of shoe stores around Dublin. One of the shops, on Meath Street in the Liberties, was across the road from Brabazon Street where Barney and Molly had first raised their children and where Patrick Ambrose and his wife Ellen had lived. A circle was being completed.

The late Sixties had finally brought an end to the money worries Molly had constantly coped with.

Compared to her other sons, Kevin had also stayed at home a long time. He was the main money-earner in the home as Barney earned a standard wage in Booth Poole and Martin was earning apprentice wages. Then Kevin announced that he and Vera were getting married.

Kevin with Vera on his left arm

"Mammy had been poor and had struggled for years," Kevin said, "and then she was comfortable. When I was about to leave the house, she was afraid that she would be going back to being poor."

Kevin and Vera married on August 20th 1969 and moved into their home in Coolock. 147 Leighlin Road now was reduced to Barney, Molly and Martin.

For a while, there was resentment between Kevin and Molly because she was not accepting his new wife. Barney went to Kevin.

"Would you just go to her," Barney asked Kevin. "Do it for me. It's just breaking her up." Molly and Kevin made up after that.

By now, Benny Dowdall was in the retirement home Nazareth House in Raheny. He was once visited by children of his brother Barkel Dowdall who had come over to see him and visit the hometown of their father.

Kevin would also visit him from time to time, and remembers that he would often find him sitting outside - in a wheelchair - with his wide cowboy hat on.

"Mam had asked me to drop in and see how he was, since I was living near him," Kevin said. "He didn't tell me any stories about his life as a cowboy. I enjoyed his company, and sometimes he'd start talking about the wide open spaces of the West. Mostly he would ask about my Dad and Mam. He had basically come back to Ireland to die."

By the end of the decade, events in the North of Ireland kept Barney busier than ever in his fascination with current affairs. What had begun as civil rights marches had turned into ever more violent clashes as the Catholic minority started fighting for equal rights. Taoiseach Jack Lynch, head of Dev's Fianna Fail party, gave a television speech saying the Irish government could 'no longer stand idly by' and demanding that the United Nations send in a peace-keeping force. Ultimately, the British sent in their own troops and events spiralled into bloody war between the Loyalist and Republican sides.

Martin had fallen in love - with film. After a year working in the Kenilworth, he knew he wanted to work making films and he wrote to Ardmore Studios in Bray applying for a job. They wrote back telling him that only people with Leaving Certificates were accepted. In the course of the following year Martin studied part-time, doing correspondence courses, while continuing work. He fit three years school into a year and passed his Leaving Certificate. When he wrote back to the manager at Ardmore telling him he had sat the exam, the manager - Dermot Loughrey - invited him in for an interview. Martin got a job in the projection room of the sound department, basically doing the same work he had done in the Kenilworth but now better paid and very happy.

His fascination with film was something that his ageing parents had to endure. He bought a complete darkroom set - and then in the evenings would transform the scullery and kitchenette into his darkroom. If Barney or Molly wanted anything from the kitchen - or even if they wanted to go to the toilet - they would have to knock on the scullery door and perhaps wait until Martin had finished developing some negative or making some print.

Martin turned eighteen and made a short trip by ferry and train to London to stay with Ethel and Derek. This little adventure got off to a bad start. Derek and Bernard showed up to collect Martin, but as they were driving him to the flat they were flagged down by a police car. The police were responding to a report that a known member of the IRA had arrived in the city. Martin was taken out of the car by the two policemen for questioning as Bernard and Derek tried to intervene. It looked as if Martin would be taken to the police station for questioning.

Then someone couldn't keep a straight face anymore and all burst out laughing. It had been a practical joke set up by Bernard and Derek with some friends.

A couple of nights later, Bernard and Derek brought Martin out for a drink. This was a great treat for Martin - a sense for him of being like a grown-up. What he didn't know was that the two had set out to get him drunk. They went on a pub crawl, and as they did Bernard - a light drinker - and Derek - not a light drinker - got drunker and Martin remained sober. The men decided on one last pub for one last drink. This held yet another new experience for Martin - a strip show. Derek went off to get drinks. Martin watched the strip show in fascination - and then realised it was in fact a transvestite who was stripping. The three finished their last drinks and went out into the cool night air. And then suddenly Martin felt totally drunk. Derek had spiked his last drink.

Martin waltzed along, singing, until Derek and Bernard had to prop him up. When they got back to the flat, the two men stuffed pillows up Martin's shirt so he could mimic his sister Ethel who was pregnant at the time. Carol had spent the evening with Ethel, and the two women had the task of making tea for the three drunks and getting them safely to bed.

Next morning, Martin woke with a completely clear head - absolutely no hangover. Everyone else was still sleeping, and he washed the dishes from the previous night and then decided to take a trip into the city. Sitting on the upper deck of the bus, he was feeling absolutely fine. Then a man came along and sat beside him and lit up a cigar. After a minute, Martin rushed off the bus sure he was going to throw up. He walked home, green-faced.

Another visitor to London - and a more seasoned drinker - was Barney. Bernard was delighted once when Barney stayed with him for a short holiday, as it gave Bernard a rare opportunity to spend time with his father.

"I wasn't drinking at all at the time," Bernard said, "but I went out for an evening with him for a few drinks."

Bernard, not very familiar with pubs in the area, took Barney to a pub he had recently been to with regard to a police investigation. Bernard ordered the drinks, and the barman recognised him from the investigation and wouldn't take money for the drinks.

Bernard felt a bit embarrassed, and so they finished there and went to another pub that he knew slightly. The barman there was an Irishman, John Clancy, who also knew Bernard through his police work.

"I introduced my Dad to him, and suddenly they were great friends," Bernard recalled. John Clancy gave them a steak meal and drinks - and refused any payment.

Afterwards, in Bernard's car, Barney turned to him.

"Can I ask you a personal question," Barney said to his son.

"Of course," Bernard replied.

"Are you corrupt?"

"No!"

"Then how come you didn't pay for anything?"

"Dad," Bernard explained, "what happened this evening would never happen if not for your being here on holiday."

Barney thought about this a moment and looked at his son.

"Hmm," Barney said, "if I was young tomorrow I'd join your job."

At the end of 1970, Martin had been made redundant at Ardmore Studios and started working for Kevin at one of his shoe shops. He was soon managing the small shop on Meath Street, and in time was promoted to manage the bigger shop on Camden Street. As time went by and Kevin's stores expanded - now with a chain of shops called Pick-a-Shoe - he hired a young girl from Harmonstown, on Dublin's Northside, to assist with the book keeping. Her name was Marian Quinn. Coincidentally, Marian had grown up on the same road, Ascal Ribh, where Molly's sister Delia had raised her family and where Mother Dowdall had briefly lived. One of Marian's jobs was to go to each branch on Monday mornings to collect till rolls and other receipts. Martin was lovestruck the moment he saw her walk into the shop he was managing on Camden Street, but it took almost a year - and a catastrophe for Kevin - before he gathered up the courage to take action.

In February 1971 an announcement came that was a shock to Barney and his workmates. Booth Poole was to close down and its 140 employees made redundant. In the wake of a Free Trade Agreement between Ireland and the United Kingdom, and following the building by Brittain's of a new, larger car assembly plant in Dublin, the economically unviable smaller factory at Islandbridge would shut down. The cars that had been made there would in future be assembled in Brittain's but, controversially, the new factory would not be taking over employees from Booth Poole's. The matter was raised in Dail Eireann, the seat of Irish government, by the Labour TD Doctor John O'Connell, but the governing Fianna Fail did not intervene. For all Barney's devotion to Fianna Fail and trade unionism, there was nothing the unions could do nor Fianna Fail would do to block what was happening. In his late sixties and with unemployment in Ireland as high as ever, it was plainly the end of Barney's working life.

"He wasn't a strong man and he wasn't a well man for years," Kevin said. "He just wasn't able for the work." Even so, all Barney knew was work. Barney had left school at the age of eleven, and for almost all his life since then he had been setting off to work six days a week. To wake before seven in the morning and then see the day stretch out with nothing to do was soon a misery.

"When Daddy retired, that killed him," Kevin said. "He couldn't bear having nothing to do. He had the feeling he couldn't do anything for anyone and that he wasn't wanted." Barney was also haunted by another fear that, given the amount of love and admiration he received from his family, seems strange.

"Daddy had visions of sitting on a bench in Sundrive Park, lonely, broke, and dying of heartache and boredom," Kevin said. "He told me that many times."

Kevin decided to give Barney work. Barney would come in to town every day to do the post from the company office, and Kevin would pay him. It was pocket money and a reason to be out and about.

"He loved it," Kevin said, "because it kept him busy."

Unfortunately, the arrangement didn't last long.

Kevin's star had risen too high too fast, and suddenly he had to start closing down shops and laying off staff to try staying in business. Martin heard that Marian Quinn was about to lose her job. Realising that if he didn't act he would never again be able to find her, he phoned her up at the office and asked her out to the pictures. She agreed. At twenty, Martin was going out with his first girlfriend.

One great adventure remained for the two people who had met on the streets of impoverished Dublin and had lived in the city's tenements and later raised a huge family in a state-built suburb of their hometown. Willie and Helen brought Molly and Barney over for a holiday in Toronto and beyond.

Willie had by then become a highly successful businessman - and had also become known to one and all as 'Bill'. Bill and Helen lived in a luxurious house. A neighbourhood couple had what they would soon also have - their own swimming pool. There is a photograph of Barney sitting by this pool, in short trousers but still with socks and shoes, looking somewhat out of place in these surroundings.

Bill and Helen had a basement pool table and bar in their home and Bill recalled a night when, unable to sleep, he had come down to the basement at around three in the morning and was surprised to discover Barney sitting at the bar and looking at the pool table.

"He wasn't drinking, he wasn't playing pool - I think he was just trying to grasp the whole idea that someone could live like this," Bill recalled.

Bill and Helen brought Barney and Molly on a trip to Niagara Falls and on to Washington DC.

"The biggest thing they wanted was to go to John F Kennedy's grave," Bill said, "so we brought them there."

It was a whole new world for Barney and Molly - and also not without its problems. Bill had booked in advance for the four to stay at a Holiday Inn in DC.

From Grand Canal to Swimming Pool

When they arrived, however, they found they were the only white people in the hotel or even in the area.

"It turned out to be a Holiday Inn in the wrong part of town for us," Bill recalled. "When we got there, everyone was looking at us and it felt a bit scary. One of the staff quietly advised us that it would be better not to stay, and booked us into a Holiday Inn in what for us was the right part of town."

It was Barney's only trip beyond Ireland and Britain and he enjoyed the whole experience greatly. Even though it had been Bill's only chance to give his Dad some taste of the new life he had built, he took comfort in having had at least that one opportunity to treat his parents to such a holiday. Bill had come a long way from the kid who had been fished out of the weeds and mud of the Grand Canal. Barney and Molly's family had come a long way from the impoverished origins of the couple living in a Dublin tenement at the start of Ireland's independence.

Barney and Molly outside the White House

Story's End

Barney, always a thin man, had become frail. Over the years, the two main problems with his health - emphysema and bronchitis - had been eating away at him and made him weaker. An unfair twist was that his body could also no longer deal with his enjoyment of alcohol. He had always been a very controlled smoker - he was accustomed to smoking maybe half a cigarette, then stubbing it and resting the butt on his ear for a later smoke. But he could no longer drink at all. Martin recalled a time when Val Loy and he drove Barney down to The Good Companions pub: he had already become too weak for the fifteen minute walk. Barney had a bottle of stout and a whiskey, and had to be helped back to the car incapably drunk.

"I saw with my own eyes what was happening to him," Betty said. "Daddy's sister Nellie was in Stevens Hospital, dying. I had gone up with him to see her. Afterwards, he was very shaken and I took him into a pub for a drink. He had a whiskey and a glass of porter - and after it you'd think he'd been in the pub all day. He just couldn't take the drink anymore."

Barney had often suffered ill-health and had fought through. Now, his body was surrendering to its years of struggle. He had become a very weak man. As his seventieth birthday approached, he was able to eat and

Story's End

drink less and less. Several of the family had come home for Barney's birthday, including Luke. There were great concerns for Barney's health, and his children wanted to be around him.

Barney

On July 19th 1973, Barney turned seventy. He was already bedridden, and Molly sat with him as he opened his birthday cards. He would smile as he opened each card - shaking it to see if there was some money inside. He opened Ethel's card and there was no money inside.

"When they go away," he said to Molly, "they forget you."

Ethel had been standing outside on the landing and walked into the room.

"I brought myself instead," she told him.

The concerns felt by the family were justified. The day after his birthday, Barney collapsed. The doctor said that Barney was dying and nothing could be done for him. The choice was whether Barney would die in hospital or at home. The natural wish was to keep him at home. A sofa-bed was brought in from a relative and put in the front room downstairs so that Barney could lie there. In the following days, he was mostly unconscious or barely conscious as his family gathered around him.

The doctor said that if the family wanted to give Barney a good send off, they should buy a bottle of champagne and wet their father's lips with it from time to time. In the last days of Barney's life, that's what his children did.

Greta recalled a time when Molly, sitting at Barney's bedside, said "Barney, you promised you'd never leave me." But it was not to be. Barney was fading.

"I got a call from Derek," Bernard recalled, "saying Dad was dying. I flew home. Dad was never a big man - maybe ten or eleven stone - but when I walked into the house I saw him lying on the couch bed in the livingroom and he was probably four or five stone. No one had told me. When I saw him, I just died inside. More than me being able to give him a cuddle, he had to grab me because I was crying."

Bernard stayed in the house a few hours, then left and went back to the airport and flew home.

"I couldn't take it," he said.

Bill arrived in from Toronto on the morning of July 26th. By then, however, Barney was barely conscious - and barely breathing.

"I don't think he ever recognised me as being there," Bill recalled.

Luke remembered the moment, around nine o'clock on the evening of Thursday July 26th, when the doctor turned to Molly and said "I'm sorry, he's gone."

Luke thought the doctor was mistaken.

"He's still moving," Luke said to him.

"I'm sorry," the doctor replied, "That's the way it happens. Your Dad is dead."

Maureen went out to the back garden to bring in Martin, who was there alone. The family gathered in the front room for prayers.

Barney's remains were moved up to the front bedroom to be laid out. Austin, still working for Kirwan's Funeral Home, was taking care of all the funeral arrangements.

"That night," Luke said, "I lay on the couch bed Dad had died on and slept there. I knew somebody would have that bed, and I didn't want anyone else to be the first to lie there after him."

There was a mirror on the dressing table in the front bedroom where Barney's remains lay and his reflection could be seen as one entered the room. Luke, knowing there was a superstition against seeing the reflection of a corpse, draped a cloth over the mirror.

As all this was happening, on July 24th, Molly's uncle Benny Dowdall died.

An old family story resurfaced around this time. Peter knew that Barney had a brother, Kevin, living in Cornwall. Peter contacted his own brother Bernard, in the London police, to find out how to reach their uncle and a search was set in motion. News came back to Peter with his Uncle Kevin's address and details on the night of Barney's death. The police asked Peter what he wanted them to do and he told them to let the matter rest.

Peter had a conversation with his namesake Uncle Peter on the day that Barney's coffin was being removed to the church. He told his uncle that he had found out how to contact his Uncle Kevin - but too late.

"I could've given you his address myself," his Uncle Peter told him.

Then Peter Duffy turned around to his nephew and said "it's a terrible thing that two brothers hadn't spoken to each other for so long, and all about something so bloody silly."

"What do you mean?" Peter asked him.

"It went back to the time when the two of them were young men and they joined the IRA. But Kevin decided he wanted to do something better with his life and he went away to England and joined the British Army. Then Kevin was told that because he had left the IRA and joined the British Army he was looked upon as a traitor and was going to be executed. And the man who had been given the job of executing him was Barney. That's why Kevin would never come near your Dad. There was no truth in it - but that's what he believed."

The strange thing about this is that Barney had often asked his brother Peter if he had information about how to reach their brother Kevin, but Peter had always denied such knowledge.

Barney, of course, had remained a committed Republican all his life. Bernard remembered Barney saying to him "I hope I live to see the day when Ireland is united." By the time of Barney's death, the North of Ireland was ablaze with violence as the Provisional IRA - 'the Provos' - had ratcheted up the bloody battle against Loyalists and British alike.

Two days after Bernard's return to London, he received a call saying Barney had died. But he could not bring himself to return for the funeral.

Story's End

"Derek took my place with the other five sons as pall bearers of Dad's coffin," Bernard said. "It hurt me - but I know I couldn't have done it."

The funeral cortége, with five of Barney's sons walking behind the hearse, passed down Leighlin Road as crowds of neighbours came to their doors to pay their respects. The hearse took a diversion on its way to Mount Jerome cemetery to pause outside Barney's favourite pub, The Good Companions. Barney's grave was just two rows away from the grave of his parents Patrick Ambrose and Ellen.

Ethel was talking with her Uncle Peter at the time of the funeral and found out only then that her Dad had fought in the Easter Rising and would have been entitled to having the Irish flag draped on his coffin.

A month before Barney's death Eamon de Valera, aged ninety, had retired from the presidency of Ireland. As part of the ceremony marking this event his motorcade went to Boland's Mills where he - and Barney - had served in 1916. Although a much older man, Dev would - like Barney - live on just two years after retirement.

On the day of Barney's funeral, the dog Sam ran away. He was found days later in Mount Jerome Cemetery. Sam never fully settled back into life in 147 without Barney. He would eventually disappear, to be found after many months as Molly was being driven along Sundrive Road and saw him with some children. She went back to reclaim Sam and the children implored her to let them keep the dog that had become their family pet. Molly let Sam stay with them. She allowed him his new life.

"I wish I'd known Daddy better," Bernard said, looking back. "I wish there would have been a time when we could have done things together or simply sat down and had a chat over a pint. I have a very strong sense of family - my family always comes first. I think I got that from Dad."

"One thing about Dad that I hope also I have from him," Kevin said, "is that he always saw the good in people."

"I never knew anyone who didn't like Daddy," Greta said. "He had a lovely way. He was such a kind and gentle man."

Greta told a magical story. She was living in Finglas, raising her family with Tom. One day, she was chatting with some neighbours and the subject of favourite, treasured objects came up.

"When I turned twenty one," Greta told them, "my Daddy gave me a little envelope and inside it were rosary beads and a little note from him saying 'from me to you'. I treasured those beads but I lost them a couple of years ago."

One of the neighbours listening to this, Mrs Kelly, asked Greta to describe the beads. Greta did so. Then the woman went in to her house and returned. She handed Greta the beads. She had found them years before out on the road.

Martin had turned twenty one a month after Barney's death, and within a couple of months of this he and Marian broke the news to her parents and to Molly that Marian was pregnant. Martin and Marian were more than delighted to say they were getting married - although everyone was saying there was no pressure on them to do so. They wed on November 3rd

1973. Brigid, who made Marian's wedding dress, was the bridesmaid. Marian's brother Eugene was best man.

Early in 1974, Marian and Martin moved in with Molly. During these last months of the pregnancy, Molly taught Marian her crocheting skills as they prepared for the new arrival. On May 30th, Marian gave birth to a fine healthy baby boy in St James's Hospital. Typical of the time, Martin was at home asleep while Marian was in labour. At around six in the morning Molly, who had been phoning the hospital during the night for updates on Marian, came into the bedroom to wake Martin.

"Congratulations son," she said to him, "you have a baby boy."

"That's great," Martin replied - and then went back to sleep.

The baby was named Bernard John - after his two grandfathers. Martin, Marian and Bernard stayed with Molly another few months before moving to their own flat. Bernard was the last Duffy baby being raised in 147 Leighlin Road, and another 'Bernard' to carry on the proud name.

Widowed and her last child having moved out, Molly lived a further seventeen years, alone, in 147 Leighlin Road.

The daughters were regular visitors to her, as was Kevin.

"Mammy was lonely," Kevin said. "Brigid and Ethel were fantastic. I'm eternally grateful to them for the way they looked after Mammy. But she was mostly alone." Kevin would visit her to 'hide' - to get away from business phone calls and demands. He and Molly had other traditions too.

"I used to go up to Mammy for every Wimbledon," he recalled. "No matter who was looking for me, Mammy would answer the phone and say 'no, he's not here'."

Molly and Max

Kevin would bring Molly strawberries and cream, and the two would watch the matches. "If I half closed my eyes at all, she'd take the phone off the hook so I wouldn't be disturbed."

Sometimes, Kevin would call her to let her know he was going on a business trip down the country and would be dropping in late on the way back.

"Of course, the fact I rang her meant she'd cook me something," Kevin said. "I would have already had my dinner. But I'd eat it - and you'd have to eat it, since she had gone to so much trouble. And I might be the only person she'd seen that day."

Derek and Ethel had returned to Ireland in 1977, and thereafter she and Brigid made frequent visits to Molly. Brigid made almost daily visits, and continued to be the one nominated by Molly to do chores around the house. Ethel and Brigid developed a routine of visiting Molly together on Mondays. Ethel remembered one time when Kevin came up to the house at lunchtime on the same day, and he had brought along a record he had just bought for his Mam; 'My Irish Molly'.

"He danced Mammy around the kitchenette," Ethel said, "and she was in her element." Molly always loved Kevin's shenanigans. If Molly said she wasn't feeling well, Kevin would gather up some of her ornaments and would put them along the garden hedge as he was leaving.

"She'd be cursing him," Ethel said, "but at the same time she'd be delighted with herself."

"I was always playing games on Mam," Kevin recalled. "It's the way it always was between Mam and me. I'd sometimes put on shows in the house as a joke for her, or I'd ring her up and pretend I was someone else looking for me. I might not have seen Mam every day, but I was in touch with her every day - and most times with some kind of stunt to have some fun."

Molly mellowed a lot with old age. She was a much more easy-going grandmother than she had been a mother - but she had also been freed from the role of 'the boss' and could enjoy her grandchildren while leaving the job of disciplining them to their parents. She would crochet baptismal dresses for all the grandchildren as they came along, and nothing was more precious to her than to hold a baby again. Molly often babysat Ethel's children, for instance, and formed a loving bond with them. She would sometimes join Ethel and Derek on holidays.

Ethel and Derek's eldest, Ciaran, became a croupier and casino manager in later life, and said he thought this was a result of his grandmother teaching him how to play poker as a boy. He noted that Molly probably thought the children hadn't noticed her cheating.

"My kids idolised her," Ethel said. "She'd sit and tell them stories, and one thing she did when they were small is she would fit my two youngest boys, Conor and Declan, inside her cardigan to wrap it around them as they sat on the couch. I'd come home after Mam had been babysitting to find the three of them asleep."

Molly went on holidays to Bill and Helen almost every year when she was still well enough to travel, and would sometimes stay for several months.

"It was a matter of her coming to us and going home when she wanted to go home," Bill said. "Mam was a great favourite with our friends who would come around to see her. She was a great character and made a lot of friends."

On some of these trips, Bill and Helen managed the very rare achievement of getting Molly drunk.

"All it took was a glass of wine or two," Bill recalled. "But she enjoyed it and we would have great fun together." Molly formed a close bond, too, with Bill and Helen's son Liam.

Bill and Kevin, successful businessmen, always made sure that Molly lived comfortably. Molly once won a cash prize from the Evening Herald and used this to buy a Parkray oven and gas cooker. It soon became clear to Kevin, however, that Molly couldn't understand the system. He and Bill had a simple gas central heating system installed in place of the Parkray and Molly just had to press one switch for everything to function. They later also had double-glazing fitted in the windows and doors of 147.

Story's End

Molly fell behind the changing times, however, and was particularly confused by technology. She was fascinated by the fact that people could own a 'viveo', as she called it - a video recorder. Kevin had gone down the dead end of buying a chunky Philips 2000 home video recorder. One time, Molly was visiting Martin and Marian and saw their sleek VHS recorder. "Oh Kevin's is better," she commented to them. "It's much bigger than yours."

For one of her birthdays, Martin bought Molly a bonsai tree - it was a genuine 17 year old tree not much more than a foot tall. Molly accepted the gift, humouring Martin, then turned to one of her daughters and whispered "I'll give it plenty of plant food and with the help of God it'll come on."

Crumlin was changing too, as the people of Molly's generation were dying and a young generation were starting to move in. One family were watching out for 147, and even came to the door because they had heard Molly was going to be moving out. Not that she ever would.

Molly was getting older, but old age needs the simplest trigger to turn into fragility. Once, Molly was running for a bus in town on her way to visit Betty who was in hospital. She fell, and the people who rushed to her help wanted to call for an ambulance. She asked instead that someone get her a taxi home. When she got home, Molly phoned Brigid. When Brigid saw her condition, she called an ambulance. In hospital, it was clear that the situation was serious: Molly had broken her hip and needed to get a hip replacement. After the operation, she stayed with Brigid for three months before going back to 147. By then, Molly could no longer get up the stairs of the house and so a bed was set for her in the livingroom. She had become frail and needed a walking frame.

Late in 1989, in the middle of the night on a Saturday night, Molly got up to go to the toilet. She fell. Long before, Bill and Kevin had given her a necklace alarm device - all she had to do was pull on this and the police would automatically get an alarm signal and help would come for her. She said later that she didn't want to bother people in the middle of the night.

Molly went unconscious and lay there until the following day. It was a Sunday morning and a nurse called to the door to dress the ulcers on Molly's legs. There was no answer at the door and the nurse knocked on neighbour Mary Donoghue's door knowing that she had a key. Mary used her key but Molly had put the safety chain on the door. Mary's husband cut through the chain and they entered 147 to find Molly lying unconscious on the floor. They immediately called an ambulance and informed the family. Molly was rushed into intensive care. She had broken her other hip, but also the shock to her system gave her pneumonia.

It was the start of an eight month slow fade for Molly. It became a roller coaster of hope and despair for the family as she would be at death's door and then make a stunning recovery. She even became well enough to have the hip replacement operation needed after the fall.

Each time Molly recovered, however, it was not to the level she had been before. She had a series of minor strokes that induced a form of senility. The hospital reached the point where they said they could do no more for her, although Molly could not even feed herself.

Story's End

Kevin and Bill stepped in to share the cost of arranging that Molly had private care in a nursing home. She was moved to a home along the same Grand Canal that both Bill and Ethel had had their spills into in their childhood. She had a bright corner room with patio doors looking out to a garden.

"She was losing weight, and one time her engagement ring went missing," Brigid recalled. "It turned out that the matron had it for safe-keeping. I had it cut smaller to fit Mammy's finger again but it and Mammy's wedding ring then started slipping off. We had to take them away." Like her mother, Molly was shrinking into a tiny, frail woman.

Ethel phoned Bernard, asking him to come home and see their mother.

"She told me that Mam had become a small, frail old woman and that I'd die when I saw her," Bernard said. "It was the one thing I couldn't hear. It immediately took me back to the time I had seen Dad before he died."

Molly had been talking to some of the staff about the crocheting she used to do, and they asked to see some. Ethel brought in the christening set that Molly had made for her so that Molly could show it off. It was stolen from the wardrobe in Molly's room. Molly was so upset that she insisted Ethel bring her in more wool and her crochet needles and she tried to crochet again.

"She tried for weeks," Brigid said. "It was pitiful to see her." During this time, Molly's daughters were visiting her every day. For Brigid, it was a particularly difficult time - her daughter Aisling had been in a serious car crash just days before Molly's fall. Brigid never told Molly that Aisling was ill, but was rushing between caring for Aisling, who needed help and physiotherapy at home, and Molly.

Molly's senility caused many problems and confusions for her and the family. Martin was phoned once by Ethel asking him to go visit Molly who was crying because he didn't visit her anymore - yet he had been with her earlier that day. Another time, Martin mentioned to Molly that he wouldn't see her for a few days as he had to go to London. He got a call in London to phone Molly - who had become terribly upset because she thought that Martin was a little boy and had run away from home to London.

Molly started complaining that there were people in her room who wouldn't leave, and it was finally realised that it was the television that disturbed her. Another time, she said she had been out on a horse and carriage ride with her brother Willie. When the sisters tried to figure this out, they discovered that Molly's son Bill had phoned and the staff, unable to bring the phone to Molly, had wheeled her bed to the phone so she could speak with him.

It was a great mercy that, as her life faded away, Molly's mind played tricks on her that brought her back to her youth and to the evenings when she would meet up with her friends to dance and make music into the night on the streets of Summerhill.

"I had a lovely walk yesterday," she once told her visitors. "Meself and Delia went down to the shops to look at the dresses. She wanted us to go into town but I said I was too tired. You know they came and took me off in the car last night. We went dancing. But I'm tired after it, you know?"

She also revisited the strange time when Barney was in hospital, their son had died, and she had found the baby. "Stop the baby from crying," she would sometimes say, in her delirious state.

"The blanket would be rolled up behind her in the bed," Ethel recalled, "and she'd whisper to me - 'am I hurting the baby? Don't tell them the baby is here.'"

At times, too, she said that Barney had been around to visit her.

"Listen where's your Daddy?" Martin remembered Molly once saying to him. "I was talking to him here last night and then he went. "I'm off now Moll," says he and I haven't seen nor heard tell since. And I thought he was dead. I did. I don't know what's going on with him."

Maybe all her angels were gathering.

Kevin was the joker to the end. As Molly was fading, Ireland was gripped in World Cup fever as the Irish team reached as far as the quarter finals. On the evening of one decisive match, as the streets of Ireland were packed with people draped in Irish flags and chanting 'olé, olé olé olé', Kevin showed up at the nursing home dressed so and came into Molly's room singing the chant and cheering for Ireland. Weak as Molly was, Kevin's antics drew a smile from her.

Molly's eighty third birthday in April 1990 was celebrated with a big gathering in her room. She could be amazingly lucid at times, and she sang a beautiful old song. It was the last time she would be with family and friends for a sing-song.

Her body gave up step by step, fighting all the way. She began to lose her voice. Molly was always telling her children that she loved them.

"I love you," were the last words many of her sons and daughters heard from her. Breda believes that Molly's last word was 'Barney'.

Molly became so weak she could barely move in the bed. Someone noticed that a dark grey streak was forming on her white hair along the side of her head, and it was realised that this was from her sons and daughters at her bedside stroking her hair.

She could no longer drink or eat and was given nutrition through a drip in her arm - with the nurses having ever more difficulty finding a vein they could use. Molly would lie, breathing fitfully but still aware, her parched mouth being daubed with water. The powerhouse of a woman who raised thirteen children to adulthood, had lost two babies in their infancy and had been twenty times pregnant lay shrunken and frail. The doctors said it was her heart that kept on going - her heart wouldn't give up. Molly's heart was not to be underestimated. It had been the engine of her life and her love of her husband and family.

On the morning of Monday June 18th 1990, Greta and Breda were at Molly's bedside.

"Hold your Mammy's hand," the nurse said to Greta, "she's going."

Greta held her mother's hand and felt her pass away. It was an inevitability Molly's children had been trying to deal with, but it was a heartache for all.

Molly was buried with Barney in Mount Jerome Cemetery. The story of Barney and Molly was over - or beginning in a new way. Perhaps they were reuniting in the next life. Perhaps they could even be with their son Paddy again.

Back in August 1963, when Paddy had met Molly at the airport in London, he had given her a brooch.

"When Paddy's Mam died," Marie said, "the brooch came back to me."

With the death of Molly, one final chapter of the family story was to close: 147 Leighlin Road would be put up for sale. The family went to the house, each taking away some kind of souvenir. One day, Martin was in the attic clearing it out and Greta was on the landing as he handed things down to her. There was a holy picture in a frame, and as Martin passed this down, something fell out of the back of the frame. It was a hand-coloured photograph of the young Barney and Molly with two children - the photo on the cover of this book. Patrick Ambrose had had several studio photographs of himself taken. Perhaps this photograph was a gift from him to them. Given the natural assumption that the couple would be photographed with whatever children they had, and given that the children are a girl approaching two years old and a boy (his clothing is tinted blue) of a few months old, this must be Barney and Molly with their daughter Betty and their son Bernard - the boy who would die within months of this photograph being taken. The photograph could very well have been a Christmas treat for Barney and Molly in 1929. Barney is twenty six and Molly is twenty two. It is the year when Patrick Ambrose told his sons, then all out of work, to sell off the contents of his allotment. It is the eve of the terrible year when the couple's first son would die, Barney would come close to death, and Molly would take in the abandoned child.

Indeed, maybe that's why the photograph had been hidden behind a holy picture - perhaps it had become a painful reminder of those times.

Smiling out from the photograph are a happy and handsome young married couple still in the early stages of their long and extraordinary journey together. Barney's hand is stretched out protectively to his daughter Betty who leans on her mother's leg. The baby Bernard has his hands clasped across his chest and looks content. Molly, a slight smile on her face, is a beautiful young woman.

All was yet to come: the future a blank page to be filled one day by this book's attempt to tell their story. We are the children and descendants of their story. Their love is the reason why we have our lives.

Story's End

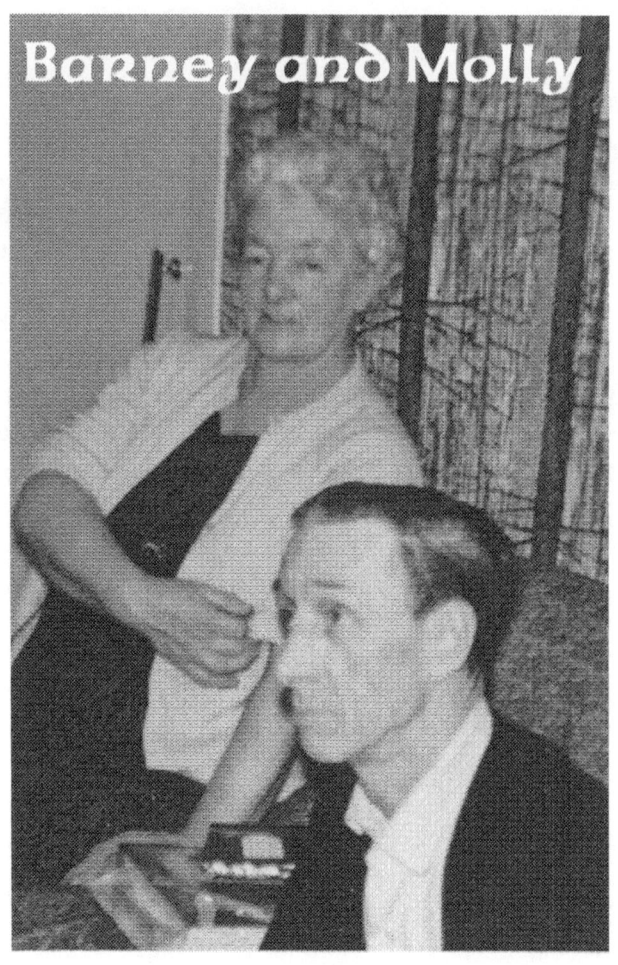

Kevin Tammany Duffy

Barney's brother Kevin was a seed of the family story that grew far from the family tree. It was Luke who rebuilt the connection to his Uncle Kevin. "I didn't try to get in touch with him until after Mammy had died," Luke said. "I wrote to the army - I knew what regiment he was in - and they forwarded the letter to him." Thanks to Luke, Martin made a visit to his newly discovered uncle in Cornwall. From that meeting came Uncle Kevin's contribution to the story of Barney and Molly - but also some of the man's own story.

In 1935, a year after he had left Ireland and his father had died, Kevin was serving in Plymouth. There, one evening in a cinema, he met the woman who would become his wife. Margaret Mitchell - Peggy - was a nurse.

"I used to always go to the cinema," Peggy recalled. "The matron always said 'go see a comedy - get away from nursing'. I went and got one of the cheaper seats in the balcony. Kevin was there and he kept looking around at me all the time. And I kept looking at him and I thought 'he isn't a bad looking chap'. Afterwards, I was walking alone back to the nurses' home and he asked if he could accompany me and I was very grateful - it wasn't good to be out alone at night. And then he asked if he could see me again and I agreed."

The matron soon learned about Peggy seeing Kevin and one night invited him in for a drink. She then presented him with a pint of milk.

"I'd never forgive her for that," Kevin joked. The courtship only lasted a few weeks. Kevin was sent off to be stationed in India. Peggy saw him off at the ship, the Redmond, in September 1935 and thereafter they wrote to each other.

"I decided I was going to follow and get married out there," recalled Peggy. But then the Second World War broke out. "We weren't allowed to go because the seas were all mined. No families were allowed out. I just got on with my work - in the war, people didn't have time to think about themselves. Plymouth was bombed so many times."

After his service in India, Kevin was sent to Burma. It would be a full nine years before he and Peggy saw each other again.

Kevin always sported a fine big handlebar moustache - reminiscent of his father's. His fellow soldiers in Burma would often joke with him that they would sneak up on him some night and cut it off. He had always warned them not to try. One night in Burma, as all slept, a soldier crept to Kevin's bunk with a scissors. Kevin was asleep. The soldier was just about to clip off one side of the moustache.

"You can do it if you want," Kevin said to him, "but as soon as you do, I'll use this."

The soldier looked down to see that Kevin was holding a knife to his stomach.

No one ever again tried again to clip Kevin's moustache.

"When he came home we got a dispensation and got married right away," Peggy said. "He was going to Austria then and we went together. I always travelled with him after that. It was the start of ten years of very wonderful life - ups and downs."

Life for Kevin's good friend Bert Hughes, with whom he had joined the army, had taken a different direction.

"Bert went into the army band and travelled all over the country. He met a very rich woman who bought him out of the army so they could get married. At the outbreak of World War Two he had to come back and joined the Royal Air Force. On the day after VE Day, he was on a flight somewhere over the Azores and crashed to his death."

Kevin's army service brought him and Peggy to many exotic places - Singapore, Burma, India. Their first child, Susan, was born with Spinabifida and did not live many months. Peggy also miscarried twins. The couple had a lot of trouble conceiving, and this was believed to be due to Kevin's duty in Burma. There were many birth defects within the families of soldiers in Kevin's particular platoon. The couple had two children: Ellen and Rosie. Rosie was adopted.

After retiring from military service, Kevin ran a guesthouse for a Mrs Bowle. Similar to his brother Barney's experience as a barman many years before, Kevin eventually had to give up this job as he tended to drink as much as his customers. That said, he remained hail and hearty into his early eighties and said the secret of longevity was beer for breakfast and rum with a twist of lime. The family eventually settled in Padstow, Cornwall.

Kevin's sister by his father's first marriage, Maggie, was living in London and Kevin maintained contact with her. Kevin's daughter Ellen remembered being brought, in her childhood, to London to visit her father's eldest sister Maggie. She remembered Maggie having a beehive hairdo and lots of earrings. She had married a man named Jackson in Dublin and they had two sons and a daughter.

"One of her sons, Peter, was in the Irish Hussars," Kevin said. "He married a German girl and they settled in Bournemouth."

Peggy and the children also made visits to Dublin. They stayed with Peter, and they also visited Kevin's sister Ellen - Nellie - who was working still as a dressmaker and making ballroom gowns at home.

Kevin never went on the trips. He told his nephew Luke that three times he had stood on a train platform to make the journey by train and ferry to Dublin, and each time he turned around and went back home.

The mystery of the story about Barney being given the order to kill his brother is one that lingered. The evidence that there was something to the story is very strong - for instance, Mister Duffy's widow and Barney's brothers Peter and Paddy all had contact with Kevin. Kevin's wife Peggy and their daughters had been in Dublin on some trips and had stayed with Peter. But there was never any contact between Barney and Kevin nor was any line of contact between the two men made by any of these relatives.

Barney's son Luke had struck up a friendship with his Uncle Kevin.

"After meeting him a few times," Luke said, "I finally had to ask him straight out about his not meeting my father. I knew that down the years several of us - Maureen and Greta and myself - had tried to find Uncle Kevin, and I know my father wished to see him again. I asked him why contact hadn't been made. But he dodged the question."

"Do you know the one with the gold ring on his lapel," Uncle Kevin once said to Luke.

"You mean the Fainne - the ring Irish speakers wear," Luke replied. "Uncle Peter wore that."

"I never trusted him," Uncle Kevin said.

Perhaps there had simply been an argument between the brothers when Barney found out that Kevin was joining the British army? We'll never know. But all those years passed without contact between the two brothers and Barney went to his grave without resolving the story.

On February 8th 1996, Peggy died. Kevin, living alone, remained active and sociable. In 1997, an event was arranged whereby Uncle Kevin went to Chester to stay with Luke and Kay, and Brigid, Ethel and Martin travelled from Dublin to spend a few days with him. It was a chance for the two family histories to cross paths again. The jolly and lively Uncle Kevin had a few great evenings of talk and drink with his nieces and nephews, and he took them all out one evening for a meal. He expressed his regret at not having been more involved with his late brother Barney's family down the years. On February 20th 1999, Kevin Tammany Duffy died after a short illness. By the end of that same year, plans were afoot in the Duffy family to bring the clan back together again for a family reunion.

The Reunion

There had been a tradition among the sisters that, in the week leading up to Christmas, they would take Molly out for an evening to a meal and a show. In 1999, with the Millennium approaching, the sisters decided to get together for such an evening in her honour. When Kevin heard about this, he told Bill. They then started to check out the possibility of getting the brothers together too - a chance for all the children of Barney and Molly to gather again. It happened.

For Bill and Bernard, it was their first time to see each other in thirty six years. Barney and Molly's children - the twelve living, their age differences spanning twenty four years - had in many ways grown closer over the years. The world of a fifty year old and a sixty year old are, after all, no different as compared to the world of a two year old and a twelve year old. Some grievances had evolved over the years, but that night such things were set aside.

At the end of the evening - after the meal and drinks - the brothers presented the sisters with bouquets. It was a lovely gesture, but also it was a way of celebrating the women of the family and Molly. It was the women who had done most to keep the family bonds alive.

The Reunion

"Every one of us grew up to be articulate, comfortable, intelligent people," Ethel said. "We have a good standard of living - in our way of being as much as in income. That was all through Mam and Dad."

"I think I'm considerate and reasonably happy," Kevin said. "I got that from them. I would like to think I have my Daddy's temperament."

"We all have a sense of pride," Brigid said, "and I believe we got that from Mammy."

"Somehow, as I get older, I miss Mam and Dad more," Kevin said. "I often wish they were around so I could go and have a chat with them."

Barney and Molly do indeed live on; the only way possible - through their children, grandchildren, great-grandchildren and beyond. And through our keeping their memory and their story alive in us all.

Barney and Molly's life together was a mix of sadness and joy. Maybe the secret of happiness is to not get lost in our share of sadness and so be able to embrace the joy. Love is surely what helps us do that. Barney and Molly were an extraordinary couple who were part of the mass of 'ordinary' people who built the foundation of what Ireland has become; a successful and confident land. I am proud to be their son, and proud to be the storyteller in the family offering this record of them for the generations to come. We can all feel deeply proud to be part of this clan.

www.ingramcontent.com/pod-product-compliance
Lightning Source LLC
Chambersburg PA
CBHW022052160426
43198CB00008B/207